Praise for *The Catalyst*

"A radical, totally original book on how to create and sustain organic organization growth. A must-read for all managers."

—Warren Bennis, distinguished professor of business, University of Southern California, and coauthor of two recent books, *Transparency* and *Judgment*

"Jeanne Liedtka has dedicated herself for years—with passion and rigor—to an inspired concept: people can build pockets of greatness deep inside any organization. Growth leadership is a choice, not a blessing from above—a choice made by largely unknown heroes who create exceptional enterprises, no matter what the bureaucratic obstacles. By studying these remarkable internal entrepreneurs, and lending fresh insight to how they achieve success, she has done the world of management a tremendous service."

—Jim Collins, author of *Good to Great* and *Built to Last*

"Bob Rosen, Jeanne Liedtka, and Rob Wiltbank unlock the secret to growth in today's turbulent and uncertain times. *The Catalyst* is a must-read book for all leaders of the twenty-first century."

—Marshall Goldsmith, bestselling author of *What Got You Here Won't Get You There*

"For anyone who really wants a practical, commonsense approach to how innovation and growth really happen . . . these guys have cracked the nut!"

—Harry Kraemer, former CEO of Baxter International and clinical professor of management and strategy, Kellogg School of Management

"The timing of this book couldn't be better. When the markets are tough and you can still grow, you've really differentiated yourself—you've risen above. This book will show you how to develop a sustainable growth engine. We've used its principles at Harris and they work."

—Howard L. Lance, chairman, president, and
chief executive officer, Harris Corporation

"Finally! A book that unlocks the secrets of the middle managers who create new innovative businesses inside the heart of big companies. This is *Built to Last* for the rest of us."

—Gerry Langeler, director, OVP Venture Partners, and
founder, Mentor Graphics Corp

"The clarity and wit with which you have crafted this book make it a wonderful reminder that we can both learn and teach through thoughtful examples—and a little levity. For me, *The Catalyst* is where *Blue Ocean Strategy* meets *The Road Less Traveled*."

—Riccardo Mascia, VP, director, and
architectural engineer, HOK

"After reading *The Catalyst* I wanted to get a copy for each of the CEOs in our portfolio. This book has uniquely identified one of the most important elements that every business must have if it is to survive, grow, and flourish in today's business environment. For those who read it, the book helps create competitive advantage."

—Jim Nelson, partner, Peterson Partners

THE CATALYST

THE CATALYST

How You Can Become an Extraordinary Growth Leader

JEANNE LIEDTKA

ROBERT ROSEN

ROBERT WILTBANK

CROWN
BUSINESS

NEW YORK

Published in the United States by Crown Business,
an imprint of the Crown Publishing Group,
a division of Random House, Inc., New York.
www.crownpublishing.com

CROWN BUSINESS is a trademark and CROWN and the Rising Sun colophon
are registered trademarks of Random House, Inc.

Library of Congress Cataloging-in-Publication Data

Liedtka, Jeanne.
  The catalyst / Jeanne Liedtka, Robert Rosen, and Robert Wiltbank.
    p. cm.
  Includes bibliographical references and index.
  1. Creative ability in business.   2. Change (Psychology).
3. Organizational change.   4. Success in business.   I. Rosen,
Robert H.   II. Wiltbank, Robert Ellis.   III. Title.
HD53.L54 2009
658.4'06—dc22   2008036069

ISBN 978-0-307-40949-2

Printed in the United States of America

Design by Nancy Beth Field

10 9 8 7 6 5 4 3 2 1

First Edition

This book is dedicated to Mr. Frank Batten Sr.,
without whose insights, encouragement, and support
it would not exist

CONTENTS

THE CATALYST

1

ESCAPING THE TERROR OF THE PLUG

How Corporate Catalysts Crack the Code

The "plug." It shows up every year at forecasting time, when your boss hands you next year's revenue target. You know where the number came from: Chances are it's been *plugged,* extrapolated from last year's number plus whatever growth percentage Corporate has promised Wall Street. And it's your job to deliver it. But despite having done all your planning homework—laying out your SWOT and five forces analysis, writing your mission statement, and conducting your competitor intelligence—you feel as paralyzed as a deer in headlights. You know you've got a big number to hit; what you don't know is how to get there.

You live in the place where spreadsheet magic must meet reality, where corporate math confronts the marketplace. You face the terror of the plug.

Or maybe, like many managers, you have some ideas about how to approach that target. You suspect that one or two of them could even turn into something big. But you don't have the data to *prove* that any of your ideas will be needle-movers for the company. And the numbers guys insist on that kind of proof before any corporate support can come your way. You are a believer surrounded by professional doubters. So you spend a lot of time doing PowerPoint presentations to convince them. While still trying to do your day job. While time and energy drain away. While the window of opportunity closes.

Now you're caught in growth gridlock, the frustrating place where the corporate entrepreneur's optimism and need for speed collide with the organization's skepticism and need for control.

Whether you're a victim of the plug or of growth gridlock—or both—you're between the proverbial rock and a hard place. Your company demands growth but doesn't give you the tools to find it. If you find it despite them, you're soon fighting the bureaucracy that surrounds you.

We wrote this book because we were tired of hearing the same worn-out stories about Steve Jobs and the iPod, the kids at Google, and the churchgoing scientist who invented Post-it Notes at 3M. What if you're not a high-tech guru or working for a famously innovation-friendly organization? What if you're an operating manager in an ordinary firm running some part of an existing business and struggling to find ideas and resources to grow it? Where are the stories to help *you*?

We knew that there *had* to be people out there like that—like you—who had cracked the code for achieving growth. Ordinary managers in normal businesses making important contributions to their organizations' growth objectives, managers who were fighting both the plug and growth gridlock and *winning*. We liked the idea of serious innovative energy dispersed at every level, lurking in organizations of all kinds. In fact, we suspected that there might be an underground movement—a kind of *Alice's*

Restaurant approach to innovation—that was succeeding *in spite of*, rather than *because of*, the organization in which it was happening. Remember Arlo Guthrie's advice to individuals caught in the grips of the army bureaucracy—to sing "You can get anything you want at Alice's Restaurant"? If just one person sings, they'll think that person is sick, but if fifty people sing, he argued, they'll call it a "movement." We wanted to start a movement.

Let's face it: Changing organizations is hard work. Inciting subversive activity among individuals is a lot more promising. So we started a research project aimed not at finding great growth *companies*; instead, we looked for—and found—great growth *leaders,* who were ordinary managers doing extraordinary things. And doing them in companies that sometimes helped but often managed only to get out of the way.

Our three-year project was sponsored by the Batten Institute, a think tank on entrepreneurship and innovation at the University of Virginia's Darden Graduate School of Business. Our research focused on better understanding the role of operating managers in achieving organic growth. When we looked hard, this turned out to be a surprisingly neglected subject. Nearly all existing studies focused either on new-product development or on disruptive technological change as the primary route to innovation and growth. While no one disagreed that managers with existing business responsibilities could play a critical role, no one seemed to be paying attention to *how*. It seemed to us that potentially significant opportunities for innovation and growth were being ignored—in particular, opportunities for creating better value for customers by leveraging existing capabilities and technologies. This type of innovation, we thought, was the responsibility of *everyone* in the organization, not just the executive team, the long-range planners, and the experts in R&D.

We started our research with some fundamental questions: Who are the managers who lead these kinds of growth efforts? What experiences do they bring to the task? How do they crack the code to discover and pursue opportunities? How do they marshal talent and other resources? Through an international nomination process in which we asked Darden alumni, recruiters, and executive education participants to nominate a growth leader whom they personally knew, we assembled a pool of 225 candidates. From this pool, we identified an initial group of twenty-five individuals who had achieved significant, organic top-line growth—not at high-tech start-ups, but at some of the largest and most established companies in the world. We interviewed these managers in depth, asking them to share with us a *particular* initiative they had led, one that they felt represented their approach to fostering organic growth. What we found were lots of seemingly ordinary managers doing extraordinary things, beating the odds to produce above-average organic growth in "mature" organizations and markets.

The following is a list of just some of the organizations whose managers participated in our study:

AES Corp.	Dow Chemical
Best Buy	General Electric
Capital One	Hamilton Sundstrand
Corning, Inc.	Hewlett-Packard Company
CPP International	IBM
Dell	ING Direct USA
DHL International	Mars Masterfoods
Discovery	Merrill Lynch
Communications, Inc.	Microsoft Corporation

National Broadcasting
  Corp.
Northwestern Mutual
Pfizer Consumer Healthcare
Power Distribution, Inc.
Procter & Gamble
Raytheon
Royal Philips Electronics

Schafer Corp.
Simmons Bedding
Sullair
Target Corp.
Trader Publications
UBS
United Airlines
United Technologies

We've since built a database that includes more than fifty individual growth leaders from a broad range of organizations representing nearly every industry and various sectors of the nonprofit world as well—enough to start a *movement,* in Arlo Guthrie's terms. We've accumulated over three thousand pages of transcripts of our conversations with them, asked them to take several psychometric instruments, and interviewed their subordinates.

We wanted to know, first of all, if these leaders could be identified by a particular set of traits that would help C-suite executives identify and recruit them. Even more important, we wanted to know if the behaviors that these people exhibited could be learned by other managers. The leaders we were profiling succeeded without any help from us or from books, consultants, or courses. They were just doing what came naturally. What we wanted to find out was whether their techniques and strategies could be *taught* to other managers. We have combed through this mass of data to distill the essence of the wisdom they shared with us so that we can share it with you.

What we learned exceeded our wildest dreams. We discovered that growth isn't necessarily the result of far-sighted corporate strategies or radical new products and technologies. Obviously, these can help: Thoughtful strategies, great products, and staying ahead of the curve all matter. But more often than not, the successful and sustainable growth we saw was driven by operating managers within a business whose leadership initiated a near-chemical reaction that generated significant top-line results. Often acting without substantial capital investments or corporate support, these extraordinary Catalysts are masters at leveraging existing resources to spark growth by creating better value propositions for customers. Who they are, how they think, and what they do combine to ignite growth in their organizations. Even more interesting, they tap into opportunities that were there all along, waiting for a leader to activate them.

Consider Kurt Swogger at Dow Chemical, who accepted the challenge of growth in a business so bad that even the consultant hired to value it for sale told him not to take the job. Swogger took it anyway and grew it into one of Dow's top performers and a model for how to innovate. We found Clay Presley, who arrived at his new job at Carolina Pad & Paper to find a failing paper company that used its out-of-date manufacturing facilities to serve second-tier retailers with a "paper by the pound" mentality that gave new meaning to the term *commodity*. Presley now runs a company seen by major retailers, such as Wal-Mart, as the go-to firm for high-end designer school supplies—and he hasn't changed jobs.

Potential growth leaders, waiting to be unleashed, exist within every business. Though some figure it out on their own through trial and error, like the ones we profile in this book, we now know how to help *all* managers develop the skills that will allow them to turn Corporate's plugs into top-line results and break through the gridlock that threatens their progress.

Having worked with hundreds of managers over the

past two years in our executive education programs at the Darden School, we've come to believe that there is a Catalyst hidden in most managers. This book, then, is a guide for understanding what it takes to find and develop your ability to lead growth in your organization. We will explore six lessons the original Catalysts taught us to help you crack the code and achieve growth from the inside out. We'll show you how to use the Catalysts' approaches to become a growth leader in your organization.

WHY "CATALYSTS"?

We chose the word *catalyst* carefully in looking for a good way to describe our leaders. Catalysts drive action. But there's more. In science, the term *catalyst* refers specifically to an agent that is *required* to activate a particular chemical reaction. In other words, chemical catalysts don't just make things happen; they make things happen that wouldn't happen at all without them. They accomplish this by reducing the barriers that would, under normal circumstances, prevent a reaction. That is exactly how the growth leaders—our corporate Catalysts—overcame growth gridlock and the terror of the plug in their organizations.

Try putting a lit match to a pile of sugar. Nothing happens, because igniting sugar requires more heat than a single match (or even a lighter) can provide. So it remains sugar, no matter how many matches you throw at it. Nothing changes. But put just a little ash on top of the sugar pile and see what happens when you strike that match. (Don't try this at home, boys and girls!) Desktop inferno—all from a small bit of ash acting as a catalyst.

The sugar is already on your table, maybe along with a ton of spent matches. Your leadership can catalyze it. And here's the crazy part: Nothing else has to change to make this possible—except you. Customers can have the same needs they've had all along; competitors can continue to do what they've been doing. Nothing *external* is needed to create growth. You can ignite it from the *inside* when you adopt the ways of seeing and behaving that we'll talk about here. You can take what is already available—current customers and capabilities—and bring them together to produce significant new outcomes. It looks like magic, but it isn't.

Because leadership really matters when it comes to creating organic growth, the challenge is to tap into the capabilities within you and bring them to life. How? By creating an environment in which it is easier to grow than to stand still. Rather than ask employees, customers, and partners to swim upstream against the relentless current of a traditional corporate bureaucracy, which often inhibits growth, you'll step out of that current and form a protected pool—using the specific practices and techniques we'll show you to incubate your growth initiative.

The Catalysts often start out in the same place as everybody else, without superior information, capabilities, or customer contacts. And then they go on to accomplish extraordinary things. And although what they do is not rocket science, it *is* counterintuitive to what many managers have been taught. The Catalysts succeed by freeing themselves from the shackles of business-as-usual in their companies. They are as distinctive for what they *don't* do as for what they do. They don't, for instance, "think big," or "let the numbers speak," or segment their market according to some set of meaningless demo-graphic descriptors. They don't even rely on focus groups.

Imagine that.

WHY GROWTH INITIATIVES STALL

The Catalysts crack the growth code by recognizing that internal organizational factors are more of an impediment to growing a business than market conditions or competitors. There's usually not much you can do about market conditions and the behavior of competitors. You can, however, do a lot to navigate within your own organization more successfully. That's the good news. The bad news is that most organizations don't make it easy. They often have two *seemingly* natural and logical impulses that gridlock growth. The first is a well-recognized—indeed, almost reverential—faith in the power of data and analysis. The second is a deep-seated distaste for anything small. Together, these self-inflicted wounds can be toxic to growth.

Worshipping at the Altar of Analysis

Organizations are designed for stability. Shareholders expect it, employees and communities like it, and customers depend on it. And stability depends on the rigorous collection, analysis, and use of information. In this environment, it's managers who know how to wield information—how to analyze, validate, and justify the use of corporate resources—who ultimately succeed. Proceeding without solid data, without the analysis to back up an idea, is a corporate sin.

But there are limits to the power of analysis. Exploring new growth opportunities always involves making decisions under conditions of uncertainty—raising the challenge of how to take data from a known past and connect it intelligently to an unknown future. It involves, borrowing a phrase from historians Richard Neustadt and Ernest May, "thinking in time": figuring out how to connect what you know about the past in order to think well about a new future. As they point out:

> The future has no place to come from but the past; hence the past has predictive value. [But] . . . what matters for the future in the present is departures from the past, alterations, changes, which prospectively or actually divert familiar flows from accustomed channels.[*]

The tricky part is spotting the divergence. Story after story, whether it is Thomas Watson's prediction in 1943 about a world market for "maybe five computers" or Union General John Sedgwick's famous last words in 1864 ("Don't cower, boys. They couldn't hit an elephant at this dist—"), demonstrates how bad we human beings are at predicting when familiar flows will divert into unaccustomed channels. But diversion is what growth is all about.

Subjecting new growth initiatives to validation through the kind of rigorous analytics that established organizations crave creates a fundamental problem: Because the data we need about the future don't exist, we have to make them up. Until we act, data from the past are all we've got to help us think about the future. So, challenged by the

---

[*] Richard E. Neustadt and Ernest R. May, *Thinking in Time: The Uses of History for Decision Makers* (Macmillan USA, 1986).

organization's professional doubters to *prove,* using today's data, their theories about some not yet existing business, managers create phony numbers based on extrapolations from the past, plus predicted diversions.

And then the games begin.

Everybody involved knows the game being played, so they deal with their fears and demonstrate their savvy by cutting the projections as they pass by. By decision time, somehow the opportunity doesn't look "big enough" to move the needle anymore. And that's a BIG problem, because the second sin in many organizations is being small.

Believing That Only Big Is Beautiful

People running big organizations—or even small ones for that matter—like big ideas. This makes sense. Limiting the number of initiatives under way increases headquarters' ability to monitor, prioritize, and sustain a clear focus. Corporate attention and resources are scarce; focus and control are key. Opportunity costs are high. Moving the needle is hard. Chasing lots of new business ideas simultaneously seems like a mistake.

But some unsavory realities get in the way of this apparently solid logic:

Reality 1: If an opportunity is big and obvious, chances are somebody else has already seen it.

Reality 2: Human beings (customers, in particular) are terrible at envisioning things that don't already exist.

Reality 3: If you insist on home runs, chances are you won't get many singles (*or* many home runs).

> **Reality 4:** When the ratio of *resources invested* gets too far ahead of *knowledge possessed,* bad things happen and heads roll.

Because of these unfortunate realities, applying the "only big is beautiful" attitude to operating managers trying to innovate and grow their businesses sets up the business version of a Greek tragedy, dispatching heroic managers on a dangerous and usually doomed quest in pursuit of the truly "big idea," the one that will move the corporate needle. Such an approach dismisses opportunities well before their potential can be reliably assessed, makes learning almost impossible, discourages trying, and practically guarantees that failures will be painfully expensive and highly visible. It almost *insists* that managers take maximum risks—in both their projects and their careers. Not surprisingly, organizations have trouble finding managers willing to chase after *that* value proposition.

Particularly tragic is the triple-threat mentality that we often find in well-funded industry-leading companies. According to this mindset,

1. We want big payoffs only: No small projects need apply.
2. Let's do it ourselves: Partners are a problem.
3. Let's keep it secret—even from customers.

When these three attitudes are allowed to drive the development of new business initiatives, the result will usually be expensive fiascos. That's because this approach keeps real learning out of the effort until it is almost too late—by fully designing offerings in the absence of real customer engagement, bringing production capacity on line without demonstrated market demand, and never giving those who are more experienced a chance to offer advice. In the world of start-ups, where venture capitalists expect fewer than two in ten projects to produce a home run, a trip to Vegas with shareholders' money would seem a far more responsible choice.

Aspiring jugglers are told to start with beanbags rather than tennis balls. Beanbags are *forgiving* when the novice drops them; unlike tennis balls, they don't need to be chased after when dropped. Which all new jugglers will do—guaranteed. As we work with organizations to build their capacity to foster organic growth, we are amazed at how often they insist that their managers juggle with the equivalent of flaming torches—assuming that no one will drop them—even though beanbags are available.

COMMITTING UNNATURAL ACTS

The Catalysts crack the growth code by ignoring Corporate's obsession with analysis and size. They are willing to commit unnatural acts. To start, they recognize the futility of the new-business-prediction game and refuse to play it. They stage a daring escape from the tyranny of data. But that doesn't mean that they reject the *idea* of data itself. They know that learning rarely occurs without information. They just believe in getting it in a different way. They use predictive data up to a point, and then they seek *real* data from the marketplace.

Second, they believe that small can be beautiful, as long as the business doesn't stay small for long. Scalability is important to them, but they *never* place big bets up front when they can avoid them, even if they can afford them. They see that the instant gratification that supposed needle-movers offer is an illusion. Placing big bets on new ideas *predicted* to generate big growth, while nice in theory, is just too dangerous in practice.

The Catalysts are willing to bet that *some* of the ideas they are working on will turn out to be needle-movers, but they believe that the only way to get there is to try an idea and allow its potential to emerge in a disciplined learning process that sets milestones and identifies key uncertainties.

Rather than worshipping at the altar of analysis, they leave the building. Refusing to believe that only big can be beautiful, they think small. They stop analyzing and start doing.

And what they do best of all is navigate brilliantly between two very different worlds—one corporate, one entrepreneurial. Like entrepreneurs, their success depends on their ability to innovate and find and build new sources of business. At the same time, they have to do this within the confines of their organizations. For many managers, this in-between place feels frustrating, even dangerous: It's a no-man's-land always in dispute between two enemy camps. A war zone.

That's not at all surprising when you think about it. Although an organization *wants* growth and innovation, many of the behaviors it relies on work directly against achieving those goals. This drives the organization's managers crazy, and rightfully so. It seems so unfair, so hypocritical. Most of the managers we work with harbor a deep desire for the perfect corporate parent, the one whose structure, reward systems, and accounting processes support the growth goals they've been assigned. Most resent the flawed parent they've got instead of the perfect one they'd prefer. It's like our longing as parents for perfect children who get elected student body president, always come in on curfew, go to Harvard, and eventually find a delightful spouse who helps turn out adorable grandchildren.

Both fairy tales have about the same chance of coming true (though some of us *have* scored the adorable grandchildren), and for the same reason. Our kids' primary objective is not to make us proud, and organizations are not designed to foster innovation and growth. Instead, they are built around the need to produce consistent and reliable financial returns for shareholders, products for customers, and jobs for employees—based on careful management of the *existing* business. They are full of systems, processes, and norms oriented toward controlling and accomplishing these objectives. Reorienting all components of the organization to focus instead on nurturing growth and innovation—even if senior leadership were willing to make the changes—is a bad idea. It would be throwing out the baby with the bathwater.

So there seems to be a fundamental, irreconcilable tension between building a new business and controlling the existing one, a tension that dooms managers to dwell in a strange and shadowy netherworld—to be terrorized by plugs and frustrated by growth gridlock.

Or maybe not.

The Catalysts don't see it that way at all. In fact, they often see themselves as having the *best* of both worlds. And this isn't because their organizations are different: Theirs are just as annoying and obstructionist as most. In fact, more than half of our Catalysts report that their corporations' systems and culture actively *hinder* their efforts to grow their businesses. But none of this seems to matter that much to them, because what really is different is *them*, not their organizations.

Transforming your organization is dangerous and difficult work. The good news is that you don't have to take that on. You can focus instead on tackling the infinitely easier assignment of just *growing your business*. You can save your energy to fight in the marketplace, not in your own organization. You *can* have the best of both worlds.

But first, you have to avoid growth gridlock.

GROWTH GRIDLOCK: PUBLIC ENEMY NUMBER ONE

You are probably familiar with the phenomenon we call growth gridlock. Picture Midtown Manhattan at rush hour. Lots of people anxious to get somewhere. Cars idling, fumes spewing, frustration building. Maybe you see growth possibilities, maybe you don't—but it doesn't matter much, because you can't make any progress on them anyway. You're not going anywhere anytime soon, because you are caught in the congestion caused by the conflict between Corporate's need to control the existing business and your need for the freedom and resources to grow a new one. If there's any activity at all, it's usually in the form of PowerPoints and meetings and lots of horns blaring. Hard to mistake that for progress, though it does chew up plenty of time and energy. After all those exhausting meetings, you haven't moved an inch.

Idled by gridlock, you—the frustrated growth leader—have this fantasy: You're an entrepreneur on your own, free as the wind. You've escaped corporate systems and processes and you've assembled your own can-do team with total latitude. You don't need to convince the bureaucracy that your idea is big enough to matter but doesn't threaten the core business. Wouldn't you be cruising at ninety miles an hour with all this going for you?

But wait. There's the problem of finding gas money. And maybe even the car itself. Established companies bring a lot to the table when they're in pursuit of a new opportunity. They start with a set of hard-to-imitate resources and capabilities. And then there are suppliers already set up, some key stuff in the form of assets, and access to broad sets of talented people throughout the company. Good companies have a reputation that might sway some customers early on, despite the uncertainty surrounding a new offering. Real entrepreneurs—the ones mortgaging their homes and employing their brothers-in-law—would kill for any of these advantages.

The grass is always greener. Ironically, entrepreneurs envy what existing companies can do, and managers inside big corporations long for much of what independent entrepreneurs can do. Then the answer is simple, right? This best-of-both-worlds approach makes sense. But how do you tap into all those capabilities, assets, and resources and still retain the autonomy to launch your new business your own way, free from the corporate systems and processes that get in the way? How do you escape growth gridlock?

It is counterintuitive but true that you don't ease traffic gridlock by building more highways. The new ones only fill up again. It is also true that the people who run the transportation system can relieve congestion somewhat by better timing the lights, designing more effective traffic flows, or just discouraging the volume of cars. You can hope for that. But there's not much you can do about any of those things as you sit idling, tapping out "Bohemian Rhapsody" on your steering wheel.

What you *can* do is figure out other ways of getting where you want to go. The Catalysts showed us an alternative route to producing growth. It was not the path of the entrepreneur, and it was not the traditional path of the corporation, either. It was a third route that cracked the growth code. This route is built on six lessons that, taken together, allowed them to break through growth gridlock, defeat the plug, and enjoy the best of both worlds.

LESSON 1: *DON'T LOOK UP, LOOK IN*

Growth begins with you. Not Corporate. Not the market. Not even customers. *You.*

The first lesson from the Catalysts is that who you are—how you are "wired"—really matters. To an individual, the Catalysts are restless and impatient with the status quo and endless analysis. For them, idling is just not an option. They hate standing still. Failure is forgivable; not *trying* is the ultimate sin.

But it's not all attitude. To quote the Cole Porter song, "If you want to have a future, darling, why don't you get a past?" Their pasts matter. Kurt Swogger was able to break through the growth gridlock at Dow to create a new future not just because he had the guts to try but because he had built a strong network of colleagues throughout the organization. Trained as an engineer (a field not usually seen as a wellspring of creativity), he branched out early and worked in just about every function—manufacturing, marketing, and R&D—and in products ranging from Saran

Wrap and Ziploc bags to agricultural chemicals. By the time he took over the polyethylene business, he'd just about seen it all. The same was true for Clay Presley at the paper company Carolina Pad. He had been a CPA (accounting is another creativity hotbed) who audited small businesses for years before moving into the stationery business. This combination of attitude and experience seems to be hardwired in the Catalysts' ability to see and chase opportunity so successfully.

But what if my growth wiring is not what it should be, you ask? Can you change how you are wired? Can you still have a new future if it's too late to get a different past? Absolutely. In chapter 2, we'll use what we've learned to help you create a personal development plan to bring your growth wiring up to code.

LESSON 2: *THE MONKEY ISN'T ON YOUR BACK—IT'S IN YOUR HEAD*

How growth leaders *think* also matters. The first step in easing gridlock is to escape the "Mother, may I?" mentality—to get over the belief that your every move must wait for an approving nod from Corporate. If you want to crack the code, stop complaining about the monkey on your back and worry about getting rid of the one inside your head. The solution isn't *them* thinking differently—it's *you.*

The Catalysts don't like asking for permission *or* forgiveness. They don't like asking, period. They don't wait for Corporate to change the rules; they elect to play a different game all by themselves.

Many managers are programmed to think "the corporate way"—to seek certainty and accuracy and rely on data to predict and plan. That approach works well when you're running an existing business where you know a lot. It is deadly in the world of growth, where what you *don't* know is far more important than what you do. Growth is all about uncertainty and how you work with it. Prediction and analysis have a place in that world, but you're in trouble if they are the *only* tools you've got.

Faced with uncertainty, the Catalysts think like lean, mean entrepreneurs, not like corporate types. Sure, Catalysts like Jim Steiner at Corning, a former corporate controller, can run the numbers with the best of them when they need to. But they avoid taking unnecessary risks, and relying on prediction is one such risk. So Steiner started with capabilities he already had in-house, found a partner to ante up the capital to produce his new product instead of asking Corporate for money to build plants, got commitments early in the process from his big customer, Texas Instruments, and managed his potential loss to what he could afford—just like successful entrepreneurs do. The Catalysts tap into the capabilities and the network of relationships their organizations already have. They don't make mere lemonade out of lemons—they make daiquiris.

Paradoxically, organizations often push their managers in directions that make growth *riskier* than it needs to be: They demand big-payoff projects that move the needle right away, keep secrets from suppliers, and share ideas with customers late in the game. But the Catalysts don't buy these risk-enhancing approaches. Neither should you. As we'll show you in chapter 3, the Catalysts get a running start without a high-risk price tag attached.

LESSON 3: *IT'S ALREADY THERE—REFRAME TO FIND IT*

A big contributor to the "deer in headlights" paralysis is the mistaken notion that a genius-like flash of brilliance—a big disruptive idea—is necessary for growth. It isn't. Now, you do have to go *looking* for growth; it (unlike life) doesn't happen while you're making other plans. But the good news is that, if you can learn to see differently, it is *already there*. You just need to change your perspective to find it, a process we call "reframing."

As you read the stories of our growth leaders, you may wonder, "Why did it take them so long to think of *that*?" Their success is based much more on thoughtful, in-depth exploration of customers' needs than on wildly imaginative creative leaps. Clay Presley at Carolina Pad & Paper reframed how he looked at his business and came up with the idea of fashion notebooks for teenage girls. Not exactly rocket science. Jeff Semenchuk at Pfizer Consumer Products climbed into his customers' heads, took an array of products that the company already had, packaged them in portable sizes, and let everybody from business types to soccer moms customize them into their own "portable medicine cabinets." Both of these turned into very significant new businesses.

These innovations and others like them are neither the dramatic breakthrough kind nor the "tweak a bit here and there and raise prices" kind. They're all *genuine* innovations but built around enhancements to existing value propositions.

There are a lot of ways to achieve growth. Some options involve more radical innovation than others; some have greater revenue potential than others. The people who call the shots on them are different. Operating managers own some of them but not others. Think of all these possibilities as different ways to *rev the growth engine.*

When your engine isn't giving you enough power, you have a couple of options. The simplest and least extreme is to get a tune-up. In growth terms, this is like grabbing the low-hanging fruit of revenue growth by improving processes, raising prices, or changing sales force compensation. These are good ways to rev the engine but won't win any big prizes. They won't land you in the Indy 500 if you are driving a Kia.

Another option—the most extreme—is to overhaul, or replace, the engine, the equivalent of removing the old business model and installing a new one. This is the big dramatic growth of the disruptive kind that Clay Christensen writes about in *The Innovator's Dilemma.*[*] Initiatives in this category—think of the development of the personal computer, the rise of the discount-warehouse retail model, or the arrival of Internet banking—usually come with big trade-offs and carry a lot of risk for established companies. Engine overhaul calls get made by senior management, usually with a lot of analysis and deliberation, the help of the folks in R&D, and often some expensive strategy consultants on the side. Like a tune-up, an overhaul is extremely critical work in organizations. If no one is scanning the horizon for frame-breaking change, the organization will eventually be in trouble. But the people who are doing the scanning should not be—and usually aren't—a firm's operating managers.

[*] Clayton M. Christensen, *The Innovator's Dilemma: When New Technologies Cause Great Firms to Fail* (Harvard Business School Press, 1999).

The Catalysts' approach to growth falls somewhere between the tune-up and the overhaul. We call it the "turbocharge." It involves creating better value propositions for customers, not just by tweaking business processes but by leveraging the organization's existing business model and capability base instead of building a new one. To succeed at turbocharging, you must play by a set of rules that are completely different from those that govern the tune-up and the overhaul. For starters, you need to know your customers very well and be able to reframe your value proposition to see it through their eyes. This makes turbocharging the kind of growth that operating managers are uniquely situated to see and execute. In chapter 4, we'll examine the formulas the Catalysts used to find growth in their businesses, and we'll work with you to identify opportunities to turbocharge yours.

LESSON 4: *SMALL IS BEAUTIFUL*

So by now you are tapping into your inner growth leader, thinking like an entrepreneur, and looking for opportunities to connect your organization's capabilities with a concrete opportunity to create better value for your customers. Let's say that you've found one.

Now you've got to figure out how to *move* that idea into action at some point before your retirement date. You've been encouraged to "think big" and to swing for the fences. Form a committee, start gathering data, run some pro forma P&Ls, maybe even hire some high-priced market research firm to help you assess the idea's potential. After you've done the analysis, focus on a big preemptive launch. Catch competitors off guard.

We've got a better idea. Try starting with beanbags instead of flaming torches. If you're a novice at this growth stuff, you're a lot less likely to get burned. Launch it small and focus on learning what works. Place some small bets fast. Find a customer—maybe just a single one. Try to sell that customer something, even if it's just a rough prototype. Enlist some advice from your supply chain. Internally, find a team of seasoned performers to give it real attention. Think of your new business as a *hypothesis to be tested*.

To accomplish this, you'll probably need to build a protective bubble that lets you escape detection by the corporate radar, at least until after there is a level of success that you *want* to be noticed. This bubble lets you focus your energy on learning in real time from real customers, rather than filling out corporate budget requests. A bubble that makes "good enough" good enough. A bubble that lets you call the baby ugly if it turns out to be. Then when you're confident that you've got the winning recipe figured out, ramp it up with a vengeance.

That's what Conrad Hall, a Catalyst operating in the classified advertising segment, did. He didn't start big, but he got big quickly. He purchased a small publication in an interesting new area just as an experiment, worked out the model quickly, and then ramped up to national scale in just two years.

Here, we will take a deep dive into a process that we call a "learning launch." It focuses on placing small bets fast, a passion that all the Catalysts share. This process aims to minimize risk, accelerate learning, and generate data and insights quickly from direct market experience. A learning launch is definitely not a test; it's an *art* that requires developing some new skills, thinking deeply about some stuff you probably ignore, and committing some unnatural acts (by corporate, not decency, standards). In chapter 5, we'll explore the magic of why learning launches work, and in chapter 8, we'll help you design one around your new business idea.

LESSON 5: *LEAD WITH PRAGMATIC IDEALISM*

The Catalysts are not superheroes. They don't try to go it alone. And neither should you. One of the key factors in their success is their ability to assemble and motivate high-performing teams. It isn't always easy. But they refuse to settle for B-team players. They hold their teams to high standards of accountability, which involves some hard choices and leadership behaviors that might seem harsh at times but are necessary for getting the job done. They are somehow able to combine two seemingly opposing forces: setting high expectations and holding people ruthlessly accountable for delivering results and, at the same time, engaging people's passions. They take risks with new business ideas, but not with people. In fact, they don't hesitate to remove any team member who isn't delivering. Yet the people who work for them describe these tough bosses as "caring," "motivating," and "inspiring." Though growth leaders like Arkadi Kuhlmann at ING Direct clearly put performance first, in the end they get *both* performance and inspired engagement. They are pragmatic idealists.

In chapter 6, we'll look in detail at how the Catalysts pull off this feat and help you assess whether a pragmatic leadership approach could enhance your team's ability to lead growth.

LESSON 6: *SPEED THRILLS*

When the five lessons we've talked about come together, the effects are extraordinary. They produce the last tool in the Catalysts' toolkit: *speed*. Speed is their mantra. Growth leaders such as Kurt Swogger not only create growth but also accelerate the entire growth process. They put some ash on the pile of sugar, light a match, and create an inferno. And they give everybody who works for them a match. Through it all, their obsession with speed drives a surprising and powerful array of consequences.

But this isn't your father's version of speed that we're talking about here. This is speed as learning velocity, the ultimate Trojan horse. In the daylight, it looks reassuringly familiar to Corporate as a source of competitive advantage. After all, who could argue against speed? Yet what it actually does is unleash a decidedly subversive force under cover of darkness. You can't care about speed and go about business as usual. And you can't get there without aligning all of the pieces we've already talked about.

In chapter 7, we'll unpack why speed works so well for the Catalysts and describe how you can use it to turbocharge your own growth initiatives.

Finally, in chapter 8, we'll put it all together and walk you, step by step, through a process for designing your own learning launch. We've even thrown in a postscript for your boss in the C-suite, with some advice on how to make your job as a growth leader easier.

Enough of us talking! Over the past three years, we have loved meeting the Catalysts—all fifty of them—and hearing their stories. They've taught us a tremendous amount about how to lead growth successfully in large organizations, how to escape growth gridlock and have the best of both worlds. We're eager for you to meet them, too. After all, you've got a code to crack—and a journey to start—to find the Catalyst in you.

2

DON'T LOOK UP, LOOK IN

____

Growth starts with the Catalysts themselves—who they are, what they believe, and how they behave. Their life stories reveal a shared set of characteristics that together kickstarts a virtuous cycle that helps them succeed at growth. At the heart of this cycle is the broad repertoire they build, which allows them to use their past to create a new future. It's not that they think outside of the box: It's just that their boxes are bigger. In this chapter, we'll examine how and why the Catalysts are "wired" for opportunity and what that means for you.

How's this for a challenge: You've joined one of the world's largest and most successful family-owned companies with a long, proud history in the food industry, and your first assignment is to breathe new life into a business named for the founder's mother. Meet John Haugh, hired from the outside to be president of the Mars/Masterfoods Retail Group and charged with reinvigorating sales at Ethel M, the gourmet chocolate business named after the mother of its founder, Forrest Mars. No pressure there.

What enabled Haugh to succeed was his ability to use his past to invent a new future at Ethel M. He came to Mars well prepared to change the game in the gourmet chocolate business, but the path he took might surprise you. It surprised us. Haugh's previous experience with candy was limited to eating it. Yet, as we got to know Haugh, everything about him seemed "wired" for finding and pursuing opportunity. He became for us an emblem of the positive and productive relationship with learning, growth, and change that characterizes all of the Catalysts.

Understanding how he—as well as the rest of the managers in our study—developed into Catalysts is the first step in becoming a Catalyst yourself. Armed with this information, you can assess your strengths and weaknesses against those of successful growth leaders and create a plan for your own development. To that end, we want to examine the underlying psychology of the Catalysts and how it shapes their behavior. Specifically, we'll look here at how the Catalysts create and cultivate a virtuous cycle of beliefs and behaviors that helps them succeed at growth.

Born in Minnesota, Haugh began his career at General Mills, spending six years there—three in sales and three in marketing. He credits the firm with teaching him a lot:

> In a blue-chip company like General Mills, you really come to understand how to think from the customer's perspective. Working there gave me the opportunity to learn how to launch and sustain iconic brands (like Wheaties and Yoplait), and to see businesses that *didn't* work, despite all the smart people and market research that was done ahead of time. At General Mills, when something doesn't work, you spend time trying to understand why.

He watched colleagues at Mills tinker with new products, sometimes launching them three or four times before they finally got it right: "Sometimes your timing is a bit off, or there's some new technology, or a new customer insight—so you give it another shot." He learned an important lesson: "You want to be as right as you can, but you never know everything—so you take your best information, and you get the thing out in the marketplace."

He left the firm to go to business school, opting for IMD in Switzerland instead of a U.S. school. Why? "I'd been working with people from the best U.S. business schools at General Mills," he explained, "and I wanted to see something different. When you're sitting with Brazilians in your class, and you're assuming 4 percent inflation and they're assuming 2,600 percent, it gives you a different perspective on launching a business. My thinking was that this would help me down the road."

Post-MBA, Haugh went to work in the hospitality industry at a French luxury vacation company, Club Med, and then at Carlson, a large private travel agency. From there, he went to Universal Studios and then on to national shoe retailer Payless Shoes. By the time he arrived at Mars, he had collected quite a diversity of business experience:

> When you try different businesses and do different things, you've got to learn a new industry quickly, so you need to get sharper street smarts. You start to get a *feel* for how business works—for how to manage people, how to spot a market opportunity, when to go faster, when to back off. I've personally benefited from being in different industries, different cultures, and different countries. It has required me to heighten my sense of feel for business.

As it turned out, Haugh needed everything he had learned. Ethel M made some of the finest chocolates in America, but hardly anyone had tasted them. The business won culinary awards in the premium chocolate category year after year, but sales were stagnating. Manufactured in a small factory in Nevada, the chocolates were available only through direct mail and at fifteen retail stores in Las Vegas. Ethel M was an anomaly at Mars—it was a small business in a company with more than $18 billion in revenues, a high-end retail business in a consumer packaged-goods manufacturer that sold to grocery and drugstore chains. But despite its problems, nobody at Mars wanted to see Ethel go. Attracted by Haugh's retail sensibility and deep knowledge of consumers, Mars executives believed that he had the right background to salvage it. One Mars executive noted: "In the past we had wholesale people who knew how to sell to retailers; now we finally had someone who knew how to sell to retail customers."

What Haugh saw when he began to immerse himself in the gourmet chocolate business was disturbing. First, his early discussions with consumers made it clear that they already had their favorite brands, and these weren't necessarily based on taste. Ethel M won in blind taste tests, but husbands still bought Godiva for their wives. It was like buying IBM in the old days—nobody could fault you for it. But then their wives put the chocolates away for a special occasion, which led to Haugh's second concern: the business was highly seasonal. "It's a good business twice a year—at Valentine's Day and around the Christmas holidays. In July, you can't give gift chocolate away," he explained. With a business model that incurred costs 365 days a year, he believed that it was essential to make high-end chocolates a more frequent purchase.

It was obvious to Haugh that Ethel M wasn't going to win by making a better chocolate. "Everybody else can do that," Haugh explained. "The only barrier to entry into this business is a kitchen." There were 2,500 chocolatiers in the United States and no agreement among consumers on what "superior" chocolate tasted like. Trying to beat rivals on taste or brand was a dead end.

By the end of his first ninety days, Haugh had decided that the current business model at Ethel M was simply not sustainable, much less capable of driving the significant revenue growth he was mandated to deliver. The industry itself was growing by only about 3 percent per year. He and his team would have to change the game fundamentally to grow the business substantially. Fortunately, Haugh had been told by Mars executives that he could change anything about the business but the name.

Clearly, Haugh and his team needed to figure out how to give their target customers—women—"permission" to eat gourmet chocolates more often and to convince them that it should be Ethel's. To begin, he believed that they needed to figure out how to intersect with the daily lives of the women who were likely to be his key customers. So he and his team studied what their days looked like, their habits, and their preferences.

They also looked at other companies, such as Starbucks and Panera, that had succeeded in turning a premium-priced product into a daily purchase. This was when they had their "Aha!" moment: They would create a chocolate lounge—a Starbucks for chocolate, a place where people could enjoy the comforts of a chocolate *experience.* To encourage women to treat Ethel's premium chocolates as an accessible, everyday treat, these lounges would sell chocolates by the piece for in-store consumption as well as for take-out. The stores would also offer a wide selection of drinks and chocolate-related items such as fondues. They would have couches and large, comfy chairs, knowledgeable staff, and information on the walls and elsewhere to educate the consumer about the sophistication of good chocolate. Finally, the experience would allow women to share special moments with friends, sitting down in a Starbucks-like environment to enjoy coffee or tea, talk, and sample their chocolate purchases.

Haugh took this innovative idea and moved quickly to put it to the test. "When you go out with a product, oftentimes speed is as important as knowledge, so you find the balance and get the thing out in the marketplace. Then you start to understand what works and doesn't work. And if it doesn't work, it's OK. You take another shot at it. You cut your losses. You call the baby ugly."

He elected to launch with four different kinds of lounges: "We're not going to go out and have one perfected prototype," he explained, "because we don't even know what that would look like." The team checked in with consumers throughout the design process to determine the best color palettes, types of furniture, and overall ambience for the stores. They also asked suppliers, partners, and the vendors of their chocolate-making equipment for input. Their intent was to refine the new business as they went along:

> We'd know within three days if a store was working. Are people coming in, are they sitting where you think they will, are they ordering what you think they will? You know very soon. And we'd test a slightly different design and layout for the next one to open. We did make errors—we knew we would. But we were prepared to react quickly and to fix them.

Indeed, Haugh viewed making mistakes as part of the process:

> You know what? You're going to make a bunch of mistakes. What you want to do is to try and correct them.

When you're younger, you don't like to make mistakes. You think that's the thing that is going to knock you off the track. You get a little bit older and get some gray in your hair, and then you realize it's OK to make mistakes. It's how you learn the most.

Haugh's customer-oriented and experimental approach paid off. The first Ethel's chocolate lounge opened in Chicago just six months after Haugh and his team developed the concept. Today there are ten lounges in Chicago and a growing number in Las Vegas. And, since his arrival at Mars in January 2004, Haugh has spurred substantive growth in the Mars Retail Group: 17 percent in year one, 23 percent in year two, and roughly 50 percent in year three. The number of people employed by Haugh's group has nearly tripled, from 350 to more than 1,000.

What drove the successful growth at Ethel M? Haugh gives the credit to his team: "None of this would have happened if we didn't have a bunch of people walking around here who are much smarter than I am and much better at what they do than I am."

But we believe that there is more to it than that—a lot more. John Haugh the leader—who he is and what he does—really matters in this story. He was the Catalyst for growth, and it is his beliefs, behaviors, and experiences that sparked the *particular* business concept that Ethel M pursues. This is very much Haugh's story as well as Ethel's: Insert a different leader, and you would have a different story. It might still be a success story, but with different twists and turns. If we look at the specific growth solution Ethel M pursues—creating the luxury chocolate experience—it is written all over John Haugh's past. It is as though each career move he made before arriving at Mars prepared him in a very specific way to find the growth opportunity that had been at Ethel M all along. But that no one else had been able to see.

His experiences equipped him with a repertoire that helped him spot an opportunity that a manager with a different experience base would be likely to miss. There are a lot of smart managers at Mars, and everybody knows the Starbucks story—why hadn't they already seen the possibilities inherent in a chocolate lounge? Some of them probably buy their coffee every day at Starbucks. But they have spent their careers as *packaged-goods* guys who sell to wholesalers, as they themselves readily admit. Because Haugh had already been deeply involved in delivering premium experiences—think of a Club Med vacation—he was able to *see* the connection between Ethel M's and Starbucks's business models. Because he knew brands so well from General Mills, he quickly understood the futility of trying to save Ethel M by brand building. Because he spent years at Payless, a nationwide retail operation, it was obvious to him in the first ninety days that he couldn't win by supporting a retail infrastructure twelve months a year that sold a product customers buy only around Valentine's Day and Christmas.

But it wasn't just *what* he pursued; it was *how* he pursued it that mattered as well. His early experiences at General Mills, for instance, taught him that he had to be willing to tinker with a new value proposition. It taught him the importance of experimentation, of getting real-time feedback from customers as soon as possible. It taught him to expect to make mistakes on the way to getting it right. And it taught him to persevere—but never to ignore reality.

We're not saying that this is the *only* way managers find growth. It is just the way that the Catalysts in our study found it. They tapped into the *connection* between their past experiences and their present situations—and in that connection they saw opportunities that others had missed. Not all of the connections were as directly traceable as Haugh's, but they were there nonetheless. You'll see them as we tell the other Catalysts' stories in this book.

Maybe another leader with a different background could have grown Ethel M just as successfully. And maybe John Haugh could have found himself in a situation where his past took him in the *wrong* direction. But we doubt it. There seems to be a kind of corporate karma at work in the Catalysts' stories. They seem drawn to situations where their unique pasts can make a positive difference.

Each of the Catalysts had his or her own blend of developmental experiences and therefore his or her own unique repertoire. But all had two things in common: First, their repertoires were without exception very broad and tended to include a variety of both cross-functional and cross-industry experiences. Even the Catalysts who had worked for just one company their entire careers (think back to Kurt Swogger, whom we met in chapter 1) had moved through a variety of functions and businesses. Second, their pasts almost always included direct customer experience as a meaningful component. We'll talk more about that second commonality in chapter 4. In this chapter, we will focus on the first.

We became intrigued by what motivated the Catalysts to seek out this expansive set of experiences. They were clearly driven from within, but the search for new experiences in most cases didn't seem to be part of a grand career plan. They were just compelled to try new things. But this wasn't about thrill-seeking, either. Nobody talked about bungee jumping or alligator wrestling. Their motivation seemed to be *learning*, not adventure. Where did this motivation come from? we wondered. Was it just their personalities—a kind of hardwiring from birth? Or maybe a set of beliefs? Most of all, we wondered if we could bottle it—and dispense it to others.

Over time, it became clear that there was a *pattern* in the beliefs, personality preferences, and behaviors that most Catalysts shared. We call this pattern the "virtuous" cycle because all aspects of it seem to work together in a self-reinforcing way, propelling the Catalysts to pursue growth and to succeed at attaining it. This cycle, how it plays out in Haugh's story, and what you can do to kick-start your own are the topics we'll explore in the rest of this chapter.

THE VIRTUOUS CYCLE

The Catalysts, John Haugh included, acquire their particular growth wiring over time. Their shared beliefs and personality preferences draw them to various developmental experiences, and then interact with those experiences to launch a self-reinforcing cycle of success, portrayed in the diagram on the following page. There is a corresponding and equally powerful negative cycle—the virtuous cycle's evil twin—that we've pictured alongside it.

We'll talk first about the virtuous cycle the Catalysts are a part of. Then we'll contrast that with the vicious cycle, in which other managers are often trapped as they struggle to achieve growth.

The virtuous cycle starts with an extraordinarily important set of *beliefs* that the growth leaders in the study shared. Most also exhibited a related set of *personality preferences*. Together, these lead to *behaviors* that are highly

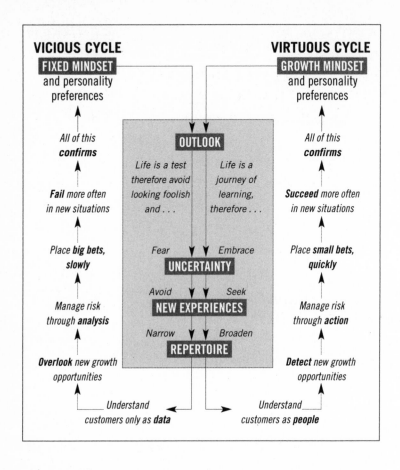

VICIOUS CYCLE		VIRTUOUS CYCLE
FIXED MINDSET		**GROWTH MINDSET**
and personality preferences		and personality preferences
↑		↑
All of this ***confirms***	OUTLOOK	*All of this* ***confirms***
↑	*Life is a test therefore avoid looking foolish and . . .* *Life is a journey of learning, therefore . . .*	↑
Fail *more often in new situations*		***Succeed*** *more often in new situations*
↑	*Fear* *Embrace*	↑
Place ***big bets,*** *slowly*	UNCERTAINTY	*Place* ***small bets,*** *quickly*
↑	*Avoid* *Seek*	↑
Manage risk through ***analysis***	NEW EXPERIENCES	*Manage risk through* ***action***
↑	*Narrow* *Broaden*	↑
Overlook *new growth opportunities*	REPERTOIRE	***Detect*** *new growth opportunities*
↑		↑
Understand customers only as ***data***		*Understand customers as* ***people***

suited to meeting the challenges of growth. We detected these beliefs, preferences, and behaviors over and over again in the stories that the Catalysts told us—and we found the personality preferences clearly demonstrated in the results of a psychological test, the DiSC, that we asked them to take (we'll tell you more about the DiSC later in this chapter).

The Catalysts' key beliefs include (1) faith in their ability to change and improve their environment, (2) the certainty that learning is *the* task to be accomplished in the process, and (3) a belief in the benefits of mutual influence, of engaging others in a joint search for solutions.

These beliefs, to a significant extent, mirror the findings of Stanford psychologist Carol Dweck in her work on mindsets.* A *mindset* is a set of beliefs. It is a particular way of looking at and thinking about the world and your place in it. Based on over thirty years of field research, Dweck has concluded that our mindset has a significant impact on the choices we make and the success we achieve. The sort of beliefs that we observe among the Catalysts constitute what she calls a "growth mindset."

These beliefs are much in evidence in John Haugh's story. It doesn't seem to occur to him that he can't make Ethel M a growth company. Even after reviewing the discouraging state of the situation—a stagnating small business with an unknown brand, a highly fragmented industry with a low growth rate, and a product that consumers think about buying just twice a year—he rolls up his sleeves and gets to work. He doesn't expect to score a victory right out of the chute. He's a *learner* throughout, working to gain a deep understanding of his target customer's daily life and experimenting with multiple options. He *expects* to make mistakes—but he believes that they'll teach him a better way. And he never even considers going it alone. Everything he does involves working with others: his team, his customers, his suppliers.

A set of personality preferences naturally connects with those beliefs. The word *preference* is important. What we are talking about here are not hardwired dimensions of personality; they are natural tendencies or inclinations. They can be changed, but it requires awareness and effort. We'll talk about this aspect more deeply when we turn to your

---

* For further discussion of this important concept of mindsets, see Carol S. Dweck, *Mindset: The New Psychology of Success* (Random House, 2006).

growth wiring, and we'll ask you to assess your natural tendencies. For now, let's just note that the Catalysts all share
the following tendencies: They prefer action to inaction,
they are confident in their decision making, and they are
comfortable with ambiguity and uncertainty. In fact,
they *seek out* uncertain situations because that is where
they learn new things. And they feel confident that they
can succeed. Again, Haugh is a great example. A boy from
Minnesota choosing to go to business school in Europe.
Why? Because it's unfamiliar, and he expects to learn more
there than in a U.S. school.

Out of these beliefs and preferences, a skill emerges:
The Catalysts demonstrate an unusual ability for what we
call "pragmatic idealism." Pragmatism (a realistic assessment of today's situation) and idealism (the belief in a better tomorrow) may seem contradictory, but they can be
powerfully complementary. Instead of seeing the glass as
either half full or half empty, the Catalysts recognize it as
both simultaneously. Our growth leaders are comfortable
living with the tension between the two; that is, they can
face the facts about today and still work toward a better
future. The pragmatism piece is key: It flows naturally from
their emphasis on learning. They constantly seek realistic
feedback to inform them about how well their improvement efforts are going. This keeps the Catalysts' bias for
action from getting them into trouble. They are not naive
optimists; they believe in paying attention to the bad
news. They just aren't afraid to pursue their dream in spite
of it. This willingness to continue to dream comes from
their conviction that the world can be a different—and
better—place.

The resulting ability to be *both* remarkably pragmatic
and idealistic *at the same time* sets them apart from most

people, who tend to lean toward one or the other. John Haugh wants to win and believes that he can transform the business, but he first acknowledges the harsh realities of customers who don't buy often enough and a product whose superior taste isn't doing the business much good. In fact, he *starts* with those realities as he searches for ways to build the better future he believes is out there somewhere.

Taken together, these beliefs and preferences lead the Catalysts to look continually for new kinds of career opportunities and motivate them to acquire their wide variety of developmental experiences. This rich exposure, it turns out, yields many advantages when it comes to the uncertainty of leading growth. Because of the Catalysts' larger frames of reference, they see more options and can vet them more efficiently.

Haugh credits his experience in multiple industries and countries for giving him a better "feel" for the business—for honing his intuitions and allowing him to see patterns, connections, and opportunities quickly and accurately. Others might call it "business acumen" or "street savvy." We use the term *repertoire* to describe the same phenomenon. Like well-trained musicians whose repertoires contain many pieces of music, all of which help them learn new pieces, our growth leaders—when faced with a new situation—reach into their cache of experiences from the past to find something that can help them understand and deal with the present. We've already talked about the way in which John Haugh's particular experiences allowed him both to assess the current prospects at Ethel M quickly and to see the chocolate lounge opportunity that others missed.

The Catalysts' repertoires usually include firsthand exposure to customers and an interest in learning more about them. Their belief in the benefits of mutual influence leads them to work actively *with* their customers rather than rely on secondhand data, like market research reports, *about* them. This relationship with, and feedback from, customers gives them real data about customers' needs and desires. Consider Haugh: He doesn't sit in his office and pore over the massive database of chocolate information that Mars maintains. Sure, he knows what's in there, but he believes that the most vital knowledge comes from interacting directly with consumers and learning about their lives as *people,* not from demographic segmentation categories. With all the Catalysts, this combination of a broad repertoire of experiences and a close customer connection is crucial when it comes to identifying promising new growth opportunities.

But the advantages that seemed wired into the Catalysts don't stop with the identification of the opportunity. There's more to the cycle. Their beliefs and personality preferences also lead them to *develop* the opportunity differently than a traditional corporate approach would dictate. Their appetite for learning and bias for action kicks in again: Rather than attempting to conduct in-depth analysis in a new terrain where good data simply do not exist, they just *try it out,* like John Haugh does. In doing so, they don't delude themselves into thinking that they've already got the right answer. They treat their original idea as the starting point for learning, and they use their engagement with customers to refine and improve the idea along the way. The Mars culture wants a new business idea to be nearly perfect before it goes to market; 80 percent and learn-as-you-go is good enough for Haugh. He *expects* to make mistakes—and he intends to learn from them. So do all the Catalysts.

Not surprisingly, once managers have entered this virtuous cycle, they're likely to stay in it. By continually learning as they go and working in close partnership with customers and suppliers, growth leaders reinforce their beliefs in, and preferences for, learning and action. They gain confidence for the next try. So when another opportunity comes along, they are poised to succeed. In fact, they succeed more often; they have to call the baby ugly less often.

THE POWER OF MINDSETS

You can't fully appreciate just how powerful this growth-inducing cycle is, however, until you contrast it with its equally powerful opposite: the growth-*inhibiting* cycle in which many managers and their organizations are trapped. A good starting point for understanding this negative cycle is Dweck's work on what she calls a "fixed mindset." Dweck demonstrates that the predominant belief of this mindset—which is all-too prevalent—is that one's intelligence and abilities, as well as the environment, are largely immutable. Life is a test, and the goal is to pass it without looking foolish or stupid. Consider how sharply this differs from the growth mindset of the Catalysts. People like John Haugh believe that their intelligence and individual abilities are malleable, as is the world around them. They view life as a journey of experimentation and learning, and their goal is to continue to develop and grow.

Dweck also observes that people with a fixed mindset believe they are only as good as their most recent performance, so they feel compelled to prove themselves over and over. Because they are afraid of exposing their deficiencies if they attempt something new, they tend to stick to things they know they can do well. They may see criticism and setbacks as indications of their basic flaws or lack of talent. People with a growth mindset, on the other hand, believe that they can cultivate their talents and abilities, so they work hard to do so. Haugh talks about his Protestant work ethic, which—since he's not a Protestant—he believes that he got from growing up in Minnesota. But we think there's more to it. Because he values learning, he believes that persistence pays off, even in the face of setbacks. Like the other growth-minded Catalysts, he embraces challenges and jumps on opportunities. People with a growth mindset are drawn where the action is and are more likely to find and apply the lessons learned from mistakes and stumbles.

When Fixed Becomes Dysfunctional

In reality, most of us move back and forth between the two mindsets, between a path focused on learning and growth and one focused on safety and stability. One part of us is programmed to learn and grow, to seek out diverse experiences, to broaden our horizons, and to actively shape our environment. Another part wants to protect ourselves, to limit our exposure to change and uncertainty, and to remain where it is stable and comfortable. We're willing to bet that even a dedicated learner like John Haugh sometimes prefers hanging out with a beer and watching a rerun of his favorite TV show to taking a tennis lesson.

Just as the organizational preference for stability and predictability that we discussed in chapter 1 can be useful and appropriate, a fixed mindset is not inherently *bad*. It can be useful and efficient, and makes sense in a stable world. But—like so many things we will talk about in this book—a fixed mindset can sabotage a manager facing the challenges of organic growth. Managers who become too wedded to the desire for protection and stability risk getting trapped in the vicious cycle, which seriously undermines their ability to grow their business successfully.

Let's unpack the difference and what it means for growth leadership.

Recall that in the virtuous cycle, the Catalysts are driven to learn and confident that they can master their world. They embrace uncertainty, seek out new experiences, and work to engage others. As a result, they build broad repertoires and close connection with customers—both of which help them spot previously overlooked growth opportunities. They then follow an experimental approach aimed at testing their ideas, which maximizes learning and minimizes risk simultaneously. Because their growth mindset makes them open to feedback, they are able to read the signals from the market accurately and adjust accordingly. Negative feedback doesn't threaten them; they don't expect to get it right the first time. But they believe that they eventually will, so they keep trying. This experimental approach, combined with their extensive career repertoires, closeness to customers, and pragmatic idealism, culminates in a low failure rate, which reinforces the growth mindset.

Now let's look at the implications for growth of the vicious cycle, which occurs when a fixed mindset becomes extreme. For managers stuck in the vicious cycle, the primary goal is to avoid making mistakes and looking stupid. To accomplish this, they shy away from new experiences and uncertain situations. They stick to things they know they can do well. Inevitably, this narrows their horizons and shuts down learning and career development. These managers often become deep specialists; they stay in one function and business and are generally distant from customers. They never develop the kind of repertoire that helps them spot opportunities. When challenged by their organizations to find growth, they are not prepared to do so, even when they try.

Dweck's discussion of the fixed mindset focuses on cognition and beliefs, but there is also an emotional side to the story: the anxiety that is, or is not, triggered when fixed-mindset managers come face-to-face with a corporate mandate for growth. Growth initiatives require a certain amount of anxiety; fixed-mindset managers tend to respond with either too little or too much. Those with too little anxiety have their heads in the sand. They are complacent and lack the sense of urgency that would drive them to act. They simply refuse to let in learning and development. Those with too much anxiety are just the opposite—they get hijacked by their emotions, overwhelmed by demands. They often respond by micromanaging, insisting on perfection or overanalyzing the situation. Their fear sabotages their own learning and development, as well as their ability to enable growth.

Too much—or too little—anxiety becomes the culprit in this story. The growth mindset, it turns out, doesn't *create* growth by itself. It keeps a manager's anxiety at an appropriate level, providing just the right amount of anxiety—the amount that spurs growth and change, the amount that allows him or her to do the things that actually make growth happen, such as building a broad repertoire and conducting experiments.

In our work with companies, we see a lot of high-anxiety managers—those who face the terror of the plug. These managers seem to end up in the hot seat; they also end up in the vicious cycle. Made anxious by the uncertainty they must deal with, they are desperate to find the "right" answer. So they attempt to manage the risks of growth by doing more and more analysis. As we said in chapter 1, their organizations encourage them to do this. To the managers themselves and to their companies, acting in the absence of analysis would be too risky. Tragically, it is their reliance on extrapolated historical data that is the riskier strategy.

When these managers finally settle on a growth initiative and then launch it, they tend to lock in to it as the only solution, so they deny disconfirming data and market feedback. They debate the validity of information rather than trying to understand the meaning behind it. They see setbacks as indications of their basic flaws or lack of talent. Their anxiety can make negative information too threatening to pay attention to, so market signals don't get through and the managers never learn how to improve their offerings. Even worse, anxiety is contagious: The team's anxiety mounts along with the manager's. Team members figure out that they don't want to be the bearers of bad news, so they often assist their managers in denying the facts. As a result, the truth doesn't get through. Until it's too late.

Not surprisingly, the combination of the fear of uncertainty, a limited repertoire, secondhand knowledge of customers, analysis paralysis, and an inability to experiment and work with feedback sets these managers up to fail far more frequently than those in the virtuous cycle. In fact, it is a wonder that they ever succeed at all, given what we know about the demands of a growth environment.

Repeated failure reinforces their fixed mindset and its warnings about the danger of trying something new. They become less confident and more cautious, which further impedes their ability to lead efforts to grow.

The vicious cycle that we have drawn here may sound extreme, but we believe that it is prevalent in many organizations today buttressed by the processes, culture, and reward systems in place. It accounts for some considerable portion of the difficulty that managers encounter when faced with a growth mandate. What is a manager caught in such a situation to do?

Go back to the title of this chapter: "Don't Look Up, Look In." Growth starts with *you*—with your beliefs and behavior. Waiting for Corporate to make the organization more virtuous is not a good use of your time.

The good news is that *anyone can develop a growth mindset over time.* The most exciting aspect of Carol Dweck's research is that she and colleagues such as Peter Heslin, who has worked with business leaders and investigated their mindsets,* have demonstrated that it is possible to alter the mindsets of both children and adults through education. Our own experiences in executive education, working with managers tasked to achieve growth but uncertain how to go about it, confirm these findings: Whereas some naturally adopt the beliefs and behaviors associated with a virtuous cycle, others can be helped to develop them. And we bet it's easier than quitting smoking or losing the extra pounds you may desire to lose. Our goal here is to help you recognize and escape the

---

* Peter Heslin and Don VandeWalle, "Manager's Implicit Assumptions About Personnel." *Current Directions in Psychological Science* 17 (2008): 219–223.

vicious cycle in which you may be caught and to learn and adopt the mindset and behaviors of the virtuous cycle instead.

True, the Catalysts in our study didn't have to make that kind of change. They appear to be naturals at organic growth. They acquired their growth mindsets on their own and retain them even if they're in a fixed-mindset organization. They get—and keep—themselves in the virtuous cycle, which accounts for their ability to accomplish what other managers seemingly cannot. You need to get there, too—and soon. If you're caught in a growth-inhibiting vicious cycle, the only person who can get you out of it is you. Everything else that we are going to suggest in this book will work a lot better if you do.

As you strengthen your ability to think with a growth mindset, you will be better able to see and seize growth opportunities. Rather than shelter yourself from change, you will develop the confidence you need to act decisively when opportunity knocks. You will become increasingly comfortable with uncertainty and the discomfort it creates. And you will be able to motivate and engage others in productive and innovative ways to turn opportunity into reality.

Just remember: Fixed and growth mindsets are not static. They change with time and circumstance. But the more time you spend in one or the other mindset, the greater the probability of your remaining there. Limitation breeds limitation. Growth breeds growth.

During the remainder of this book, we'll explore many other aspects of the virtuous cycle that we've outlined here: connecting with customers, learning in action, treating new business ideas as starting points, and scanning for disconfirming data. But first, we want to look more closely at the aspect of the growth cycle that forms the foundation for the ability to recognize new opportunities: repertoire.

REPERTOIRE

A key theme in John Haugh's story is the extent to which his past equips him to enable growth. This is true of all the Catalysts. Their broad repertoires lie at the heart of their success as growth leaders. At first glance, this may not seem noteworthy. After all, sophisticated organizations already *know* that a manager's previous experiences matters. Everyone looks for managers with the right "seasoning" for important jobs. HR departments carefully lay out career development tracks for high-potential young employees. Corporations like General Electric have even recognized the importance of the kind of cross-functional and cross-business exposure that we've talked about, and they design rotational programs to ensure that their executives are exposed to various businesses. So what's new here?

What is new is that our study demonstrates that these broad career experiences aren't just nice to have, the icing on the cake for a well-rounded executive. That may be true when we are grooming people for the stable side of the business. But if we want to groom them to be growth leaders, lots of experiences are not just nice to have—they are *essential*.

Learning theorist Donald Schön was the first to describe the central role of repertoire in the success of professionals such as architects, physicians, and psychiatrists.*

---

* Donald Schön, *The Reflective Practitioner* (Basic Books, 1983).

Masters in those fields build up a collection of images, ideas, examples, and actions over the course of their careers. They can then draw on this collection as they confront each new situation. By midcareer, there aren't many truly new situations. Chances are a version of anything that looks new is already represented in their repertoire and is quickly accessible. So what looks to an outsider like an intuitive flash of insight on their part is most often the result of a deep repertoire that allows these professionals to identify the shape of a seemingly new problem or opportunity instantaneously. This, in turn, enables them to fast-forward, again through an extensive repertoire, to find a hypothesized solution. They accomplish this with a level of speed and accuracy that renders the process almost invisible—and impossible for a novice to replicate.

Think of the difference between a master architect and a novice architect, both confronted with the challenge of situating a building on a particularly tricky slope. Odds are that although neither of them has ever put a building on *this* very slope, the master has put many buildings on many slopes, some of which resemble the one at hand. Because of this experience, the master can quickly flip through his or her mental rolodex of possibilities and most likely suggest a far better one to start off with—and accomplish this first stage far more rapidly— than the novice can. It's not that the novice is necessarily less capable. He or she may in fact be a better designer, but the novice has fewer examples of similar problems and solutions. The novice has to start from scratch and create a new solution. The master simply summons one from his or her repertoire. The master's advantages are twofold: He or she can summon a hypothetical solution more quickly, and the one he or she summons is likely to be a superior first try. That is exactly how the Catalysts' broad repertoires operate as they look for and develop growth opportunities.

We have traditionally valued deep expertise in business, the kind that makes it possible to solve a particular problem very well. This is, of course, essential to produce consistency and quality and to achieve competitive advantage in a stable environment. But there is a downside if all we've got is that kind of expertise. The more we do one thing over and over, the more it becomes worked into our brains as the *only* way to do it. Paradoxically, the more we do that one thing in one way, the more it limits our ability to do it any other way or even to see the alternatives. That is the trap of the single-business or single-function perspective, the reason why the mental models of "how we do things around here" are so damaging to innovation. It's also why people whose job exposes them to multiple industries have a leg up, and why we find CPAs like Clay Presley, who work in a field not traditionally seen as a breeding ground for innovators, among our Catalysts.

People generally see only what they have already seen. Telling someone to think outside the box does not induce creativity. Our box is all we've got. Mark O'Neill is a growth leader who runs Kelvingrove, a premier public museum in Glasgow, Scotland, often described as representing "the future of museums." He observed:

> Telling people to do "innovation" that's radically new and different—that's intimidating. Come up with something you've never thought of before. How can people come up with something they've never thought of before?

The Catalysts do indeed have bigger boxes, and they constructed them on their own.

Sanjiv Yajnik of Capital One is a great example of how Catalysts continually broaden their repertoires and then use them to grow a business. He built his leadership skills over many years in such diverse areas as marine engineering at Mobil Oil, manufacturing and restaurant operations at PepsiCo, and retail at Circuit City. Arriving at Capital One in risk management, he jumped at the chance to build up the company's small-business services. "I just gravitated to the biggest general management challenge I could find," he says about his career. "I have always been attracted to finding solutions that make a difference."

Yajnik integrated and capitalized on the skills he had acquired throughout his career to drive results at Capital One. From his days as an engineer, he learned discipline, project management, and problem resolution, as well as the importance of finding the right time to take risks. From his time with PepsiCo, he learned business management, the need for a clear vision, and how to drive relentlessly to the goal. And at Circuit City, he gained an appreciation for the art of merchandising and marketing, along with the need to understand the broader context of customer behavior and satisfaction. He used all of these to turn small-business services into one of Capital One's highest growth areas.

Jeff Semenchuk also took a seemingly long and winding road to his role as growth leader at Pfizer Consumer Healthcare. Over the course of his career, Semenchuk worked in marketing, sales, IT, finance, manufacturing, supply chain, human resources—in a variety of industries. But he didn't just fall into these positions. He went looking for them.

Early on, Semenchuk accepted a job with consulting firm Arthur Andersen and Company (now Accenture), which was starting what would become its change management practice. During his three years there, Semenchuk focused on projects that were either cross-industry or cross-functional, building an expansive network of contacts while learning how to get something done without organizational authority, power, or budgets. Eager to meet new people and explore different businesses and industries, Semenchuk left Andersen for a graphics design firm of only six people. Working side by side with the company's president, Semenchuk honed his growth leader skills while lending enthusiasm and ideas to the business. To date in his career, Semenchuk has been involved in starting up four new businesses, three of which succeeded. Yet he maintains that he learned the most from the one that failed. Those experiences taught Semenchuk the value of having, as he puts it, "a real passion for what you're doing, and a real sense of whether there's a market and the quickest way to get to it." All of these experiences became part of his repertoire and were integral to his ability to work with the myriad Pfizer brand managers, suppliers, and retailers it took to pull off the creation of the winning Mosaics business concept: customized, portable medicine cabinets for home and travel.

Semenchuk has since moved to Citigroup, where he heads growth ventures and innovation for the consumer business. We have no doubt that he is applying what he learned throughout his career to develop growth initiatives and groom the next generation of leaders there, and to continue developing his own repertoire. As he tells it, "The most successful innovation executives for the next ten years are going to be ones who jump from industry to industry. It's very difficult to be an innovation leader having grown up only within your own industry, because you're blind."

You might be wondering if such frequent job and

career changes raise a red flag. If the changes are mindless job hopping, this might indeed be true. But repertoire building that reflects the demands of today's complex and fast-paced business environment is a distinct advantage, not a liability. The difference between job hopping and repertoire building may be tough to see when you're looking at the résumé of a young manager. But on the résumé of a midcareer professional, it's easier to spot the difference between a series of different jobs and a track record of successes.

You don't have to change companies to acquire a broad repertoire. Remember Kurt Swogger, who spent thirty-five years at Dow? He built a diversified résumé in a single company. John Wallace, one of our Catalysts, who opened up new media channels at NBC, did the same thing at General Electric. And Jim Steiner, whom you'll learn more about in our next chapter, did it at Corning.

The Catalysts in our study are, like you, the product of accumulated experiences. The broader and more diverse your experiences, the more you have to draw on as a growth leader. The more rich and varied your collection of skills, the better able you are to see and execute growth initiatives in your organization.

That's interesting and helpful news, you might say—if I'm thirty years old. But what if I'm a midcareer manager and a little long in the tooth to start jumping into corporate rotational programs? Is it too late for me? We believe that you can have a future as a growth leader, even if it's too late to acquire a broadly cross-functional past. Let's look at how.

HOW ARE *YOU* WIRED FOR GROWTH?

Whatever your experience to date, you can unleash the growth leader lying dormant inside you, whether that means reframing how you think about change, reorienting your beliefs about learning and growth, or developing new ways to think and act as a leader. You can start from where you are.

Every manager can become a better growth leader through education and practice. So if you're thinking, "I'm not a growth leader," "I don't have a growth mindset," "My experience isn't very diverse," or "My repertoire of skills is too limited," *don't worry*. Whatever your starting point, you can develop or strengthen your growth leadership muscle. You need only to exercise it. Now we'll look at how.

Adopt a Growth Mindset

The process begins with developing a growth mindset. If you're operating in a fixed mode, until you consciously acknowledge that fact, you're like the proverbial fish who doesn't even know that what it's swimming in is water. The first step is awareness. It's about continually asking, "What kinds of thoughts am I having right now—fixed or growth—and what kinds of thoughts do I need to be having to most effectively lead this growth initiative?" By asking those questions, you trigger the mind into self-observation instead of operating on autopilot, driven by past patterns.

The second step is investigation. Ask yourself, "*Why* am I having these thoughts?" The goals are to know yourself at a deep level—to identify the negative stories you've been telling yourself, to see patterns in your past that may have prevented you from learning and growing, and to stretch yourself into the unknown. Another goal is to spot times when too little or too much anxiety has gotten in your way, and to realize how past experiences might scare you about becoming a growth leader today. By exploring what keeps you in a fixed mindset, you start to release the logjam and move more consistently into a growth mindset.

The third step is detachment. Moving from a fixed to a growth mindset is easier when you don't focus only on outcomes. Try to be more committed to the journey than the end result, to live in the present, to have the courage to try new things, to challenge yourself in thinking and acting in new ways—without being preoccupied by the outcome or what others might think. By taking the ego out of the pursuit of growth, you build confidence in yourself and enjoy the ride. Here is where you need to rewrite the story that you tell yourself. The new story is about getting comfortable with discomfort.

As you try to identify when you might be overtaken by a fixed mindset, ask yourself these questions:

- Do you consider your ideas as fully formed or as starting points?
- When confronted with disconfirming data, do you find yourself debating the data's validity or trying to understand them?
- Do you measure your progress relative to others or to your own improvement?
- How do you handle setbacks? As signals to abandon ship or as opportunities to learn and to try something different?

Your brain is designed to develop new circuitry, to rewire itself, based on new thoughts and behaviors. Here are some tips to help you get started:

- Find some quiet time every day for reflecting and asking questions about what you're thinking and why.
- When you find yourself in a fixed mindset, ask if it is coming from a sense of complacency, a discomfort with change, a feeling of impatience, or a fear of making mistakes.
- Make it a priority to learn or try something new every day.
- Ask questions more often than you give answers.
- Do something that stretches you beyond your current capabilities at least once a week.
- Imagine what success looks and feels like on a regular basis, especially when it seems like it's out of your reach.

WORKING WITH YOUR PERSONALITY PREFERENCES

We talked earlier about personality preferences and the way in which growth leaders leverage their ways of inter- acting with others to lead change successfully. To get our arms around this important dimension of being a growth leader, we had our own growth leaders take the DiSC Lead- ership Profile, a psychological assessment used in business that has been taken by over 40 million people and vali- dated over the last fifty years.

Designed to assess how people perceive and work within their environment, the instrument divides individual behavior into four *dimensions* that everyone exhibits to a greater or lesser degree: Dominance, Influence, Steadfastness, and Conscientiousness. There is no single mix of dimensions that is inherently right or best; each dimension competes with and complements the other three. We were particularly interested in how the Catalysts compared with broader groups of executives and other businesspeople who had taken the assessment.

First, let's take a high-level look at the key qualities associated with leaders who have high scores in each dimension:

- *High Dominance (D)* leaders focus on action and results, and are inspired by challenges and competition. They are the people who jump at the chance to lead a new project or do something on their own. They are the ardent problem solvers who often think that quick results are the best, and sometimes only, measure of success. While their self-confidence makes high Ds decisive, it can also make them aggressive and controlling.

- *High Influence (I)* leaders focus on people and on creating a motivating environment, and are inspired by collaborative efforts. They are sociable and openly enthusiastic, and are the ones who try to talk you into or out of something, most of the time with genuine interest in your point of view. Although they may lack the quick decisiveness of high Ds, the high Is are great team builders and team players. But they are not pushovers.

- *High Steadfastness (S)* leaders focus on consistent performance, loyalty, and stability, and are more reactive than proactive in their behavior. They are quick to lend a helping hand or a sympathetic ear and are always dependable and consistent. But they often take cooperation to extremes, sacrificing their own needs for the good of the group or to avoid conflict and confrontation. Their ability to remain calm and patient in the midst of chaos helps maintain stability.

- *High Conscientiousness (C)* leaders focus on systematic analysis, accuracy, and getting things right the first time. Like high S leaders, they are more reactive than proactive. They are the ones who can be counted on to ensure accuracy, quality, and adherence to standards. They are easily recognized by their unrelenting attention to detail and constant need for the facts, which can either save or ruin the day, depending on your point of view.

So what do you think we learned about the Catalysts? Take a look at their scores compared with those of other executives, salespeople, and the general population:

AVERAGE DiSC SCORES OF CATALYSTS COMPARED TO OTHER GROUPS
(Scale: 1 to 7)

	The Catalysts	Executives	Sales People	General Population
Dominance	6.3	5.4	4.8	4.5
Influence	5.1	4.1	5.1	4.0
Steadfastness	1.9	2.5	2.9	3.4
Conscientiousness	2.5	4.0	3.5	4.3

While folks in the three other groups display fairly equal amounts of the four dimensions, the Catalysts are all about the highs and the lows—even more so than most executives. First, they score exceptionally higher than the other groups in the Dominance and Influence dimensions, reinforcing our view that Catalysts see themselves as having extraordinary power over their environment, able to master and shape the world around them by overcoming opposition and by influencing others. Second, they score markedly lower than other groups in Steadfastness and Conscientiousness, confirming our finding that they have less interest in, and need for, predictability and perfection. To them, in fact, striving for perfection is completely at odds with acting quickly and decisively.

We believe these results are significant and would suggest that you first take the DiSC to get a concrete fix on your own behavioral preferences. This can be done via the Web. Once you have completed the instrument (which takes about fifteen minutes), you will receive a personalized report on your profile. At that point, consider the questions below:

- Which of the four DiSC dimensions did I score highest on, and what qualities of that dimension best describe my behavioral style?
- What are the strengths of my highest-scoring dimension, and how can I use them to my advantage as a growth leader?
- What are the limitations of this dimension, and how can I use them to my advantage as a growth leader?
- In which dimensions am I similar to the Catalysts, and what can I do to leverage those dimensions for greater success?
- In which dimensions am I different from the Catalysts, and how can I manage those dimensions to maximize my success?

The goal is to move from a leadership style of control and reactivity to one of mastering and shaping your environment. Let go of self-doubt, begin to see yourself as bigger than the situations you face, and fully embrace your personal power instead of assuming that you are powerless to effect change. The ability to master and shape the environment is critical to successful growth leadership. Here are some tips to help you move in this direction:

- Utilize the energy created by anxiety as a positive force for change.
- Practice acting with confidence and courage, even when you don't feel confident or courageous, until you really do.
- Don't wait for the right time, get bogged down in analysis, or look for guarantees; just *do* it.
- Be willing to learn as you go instead of thinking you have to know everything before you start.
- Develop a leadership style that works for you by playing to your strengths and surrounding yourself with people who compensate for your vulnerabilities.

As you think about what to do differently, pay particular attention to your Influence skills from the DiSC. Work on them if they fall below the moderate end of the scale. These are crucial to growth leadership and are the Achilles' heel of many of the managers we work with.

Expand Your Repertoire

Repertoire plays a central role in a growth leader's success. Over their careers, Catalysts accumulate images, ideas, examples, and actions that they can explicitly draw on as they confront new situations.

To determine where you are in building your repertoire, consider the following:

- Make a list of all of the key positions you've held. For each, include the organization, the functional area, and the two to three experiences that gave you the most new perspectives and skills.
- Now assess the list and look for themes, areas of concentration, and broad capabilities you've developed.
- Drill down on one or more specific experiences by asking these questions: What was the challenge or opportunity? What were my options? What did I do? What were the results? What did I learn?
- Next, look for what's missing: What are the industries, functions, and experiences I need more of to lead current and future growth initiatives?

The goal here is to move from a limited exposure to more diverse experience in your career by stepping outside your comfort zone (fortunately, it gets easier with practice). Practice the tips below:

- Examine different businesses and industries directly by working for them, or indirectly by researching them on the Internet or in forums where they are represented.
- Seek out and get to know different kinds of people inside and outside your organization.
- Look for patterns and interconnections among seemingly disparate ideas, functions, people, and options, and then build on them.
- Seek to understand the context of problems and opportunities and keep the big picture in mind. If

things start to fall apart, find a common thread you can use to weave things together.

- Expose yourself to entrepreneurial thinking by talking to entrepreneurs, participating in start-up initiatives, and reading about or attending conferences on entrepreneurship.
- Take on different roles within the organization for which you currently work.
- Learn from failures and successes and apply what you learn.

You can expand your repertoire by making a commitment to expand your knowledge and expertise. This will broaden your options and capabilities to address problems, take advantage of opportunities, and lead growth initiatives. Give up the notion that you have to be good at everything you do and that sticking with what you know or what feels familiar will keep you from experiencing pain or disappointment.

We believe there is a successful growth leader inside everyone. And we know a lot about what one looks like. We challenge you to find and develop that unique set of qualities inside you—a growth mindset, an action bias, and a broad repertoire—to maximize your success.

3

THE MONKEY ISN'T ON YOUR BACK—IT'S IN YOUR HEAD

The Catalysts know that the real monkey isn't Corporate on their backs. It's Corporate in their heads. Organizations teach their managers to think in terms of prediction and analysis, but managers trying to navigate the uncertain world of growth need to think more like entrepreneurs. Like successful entrepreneurs, the Catalysts insist on creating the future rather than trying to predict it. They employ tactics that maximize their control and minimize risk. In this chapter, we'll look at how their approach allows them to achieve the best of both worlds—corporate and entrepreneurial—and push through the growth gridlock that often thwarts new opportunities.

Jim Steiner would be the first to admit that, until recently, he was an unlikely candidate to be profiled as an extraordinary growth leader. A twenty-two-year veteran of Corning, a global manufacturer of industrial and scientific glass products, Steiner joined the firm after business school as a controller and stayed in that role for the next decade. People at Corning came to think of him as the cost-cutting guy, the one who knew how to keep the lid on spending in a mature business. Now, after growing several small businesses within the company, he's known as the entrepreneurial guy.

The story of Steiner's—and his business unit's—transformation begins in 2000, when, hankering for more accountability, he took on the role of general manager of Corning's oldest division, Specialty Materials. Unlike other divisions at Corning, Specialty Materials was a collection of smaller businesses, such as photonics, telescope mirrors, and tubing components for home, display, and automotive lighting products.

After record profitability in 2000, the group was hit hard by the telecom market collapse. "We went from extremely profitable in 2000 to significantly unprofitable by 2003," Steiner told us. "We almost halved in size and were losing a lot of money; we were stuck with businesses with very mature products," he recalled. "And we knew we had to diversify or we probably wouldn't exist." The outlook was bleak.

Steiner's response was to assemble a multidisciplinary team to consider the possibilities for Specialty Materials. "We had a basic theory that we had very broad capabilities that were being underutilized," Steiner said. "So we did an inventory of our skills with the team, and we created criteria for what kinds of industries would be attractive to us": industries with strong growth rates that would draw on Corning's existing technologies and contacts. From this screening process emerged a short list: aerospace, defense, and display.

Steiner knew that they would be playing a different game than the rest of the organization: "Most divisions at Corning are $500 million businesses oriented toward home runs. They are not interested in small opportunities, particularly those that cross divisional lines." Steiner's team, however, was willing to pursue projects that appeared to have more modest potential. "My division flies a little bit under the radar," he said. "Corning is a four-billion-in-revenue company and we're four hundred million of it. We don't get any external attention." Less attention allowed Steiner and his team more freedom and flexibility. "Because we're building off existing capabilities, nothing we do takes a huge amount of new money," Steiner said. "The tougher part is finding the opportunity."

For years, Specialty Materials had been supplying the raw glass used in about 50 percent of all front-projection business projectors and rear-projection televisions. Steiner's group provided raw glass to a third party that produced a "window," which Texas Instruments (TI) then packaged into its digital light processing (DLP) technology. "The value of the window is in the range of twenty to forty dollars," Steiner said, "and we were selling the raw material for about ten cents a glass." Steiner's team wondered whether there was a way to move further up this value chain.

The opportunity materialized during a visit to the Consumer Electronics Show in early 2003, where Steiner learned that TI was unhappy with its supplier of DLP windows. TI suggested that Steiner and his team develop the product themselves. "This is a level of value that Corning typically wouldn't do," Steiner recalled, noting Corning's long tradition as a volume raw-material supplier. To execute this new proposition, Corning would make the glass, seal it to a frame, and then polish and coat it. "In our inventory of skills, we found that we had all the skills throughout Corning but not necessarily in our division," Steiner said. "So we pulled all those skills together, made a couple prototypes, and TI liked them. We had a great team that was able to find the resources and get them committed. People like to work on this type of project because they can see their personal impact so much more."

In addition to having all the skills within Corning, Steiner saw that much of the necessary equipment was also in place, left over from the company's work on photonics and semiconductors before the telecom crash. Existing alliances also came into play: TI insisted that all DLP production be situated in China, so Steiner leveraged one of Corning's Chinese partnerships to do the production. "We also got TI to commit to a certain amount of volume when we started," Steiner said. Within the first year of launching the DLP product, Corning Specialty Materials generated $50 million in sales; by its second year, revenues had grown to $80 million. Corning ended up displacing TI's number one supplier.

More than anything else, Steiner attributed the success to a sense of self-reliance: "I think the belief in ourselves allowed us to keep chasing stuff for the future when we could have just cost-reduced ourselves back to breakeven," he said. "I used to tell my boss that anybody can get us back to breakeven. But to do it and build a future is much tougher."

It turned out that Steiner grew himself along with his business, and he learned how to adjust his data needs to the unavoidable uncertainty the world of growth entailed:

> My competencies were in optimizing a mature business for cost control. And now I know how to lead an organization that is going after new stuff. I've learned how to go forward on less information than I'd like.

Jim Steiner has never been an entrepreneur, but he thinks and acts like one. That is true for all the Catalysts: They mirror the way that highly successful entrepreneurs look at the world, and they employ tactics very similar to those used by veteran entrepreneurs. They pursue opportunities that build on the capabilities and resources they already have; instead of predicting uses for a new offering and forecasting a market for it, they find someone early on willing to become an actual customer and to provide real data; and, along the way, they never invest more than they can safely lose.

Breaking the mold, they use these tactics to succeed in large corporations, which often encourage—or require—managers to think and act in decidedly *non*entrepreneurial ways. Jim Steiner, like all the Catalysts, lives in two worlds and knows how to get the best of both of them.

To understand what this entrepreneurial thinking looks like in practice, and to discover what truly sets entrepreneurs apart, we must first dispel the myths that surround them.

THE MYTHS ABOUT ENTREPRENEURS

Asked to describe people who build businesses from scratch, most of us would use a predictable list of words such as *independent, bold, brash,* and *impulsive.* We might also call them *gamblers, cowboys,* or *mavericks.*

But research into the behavior and characteristics of successful serial, or so-called expert, entrepreneurs—people who succeed in building not just one but multiple successful businesses—shows that *none* of these characteristics distinguishes successful entrepreneurs. In fact, entrepreneurs are, on average, no more independent, bold, impulsive, or risk-seeking than the rest of us. What *does* distinguish highly successful entrepreneurs is how they approach uncertainty and, therefore, how they start a business.

Let's look at two opposite approaches to handling uncertainty.

One way is trying to *predict* the future. We can forecast industry trends, run focus groups, and estimate market growth rates. We can make educated guesses about what customers will buy, what supply chain partners will want to sell, whether new technologies will increase or decrease costs, and what our competitors will do next. We can try to figure out, to paraphrase hockey great Wayne Gretzky, where the puck is headed and skate in that direction. People who follow this approach believe that if they can predict the future, they can then control it.

The opposite approach is trying to *shape* the future, to create it ourselves instead of watching it unfold. We can take what we know how to do and then listen closely to potential customers about how to use it to better serve their needs. We can persuade one of those potential customers to work with us and thereby develop a new market. We can forget about trying to make predictions, because to the extent that we can shape the future, there is no need to predict it.

Neither approach is good or bad, right or wrong. Nor are they mutually exclusive. But most of us tend to rely on one approach much more than the other. "Predictors" like to dig into market research, see what trends are likely to push into the future, study competitors and anticipate their moves, and evaluate technologies and bet on the ones that seem most likely to succeed. "Shapers" prefer to act, to figure out what they can *do today* to make something happen and to build on what and who they already know— while remaining open to surprises along the way.

In designing this study we relied on research, led by Professor Saras Sarasvathy at Darden, on the decision-making approaches of expert entrepreneurs: individuals who have at least ten years of experience as entrepreneurs and have achieved major successes in their ventures. This research demonstrates that expert entrepreneurs share a strong belief that to the extent that they can shape the future, there's no need to predict it. Expert entrepreneurs also think about means and ends in a distinctive way. Starting a new business, as they see it, is not about pursuing an opportunity regardless of resources. The question they ask is not "What means do I need to accumulate in order to achieve certain ends," but "What ends can I create with the means I already have?" To diagnose this thinking, researchers created new-venture scenarios with varying levels of uncertainty, presented them to more than one thousand entrepreneurs and venture investors, and then evaluated how they approached decision making as they worked through the scenarios.

The growth leaders study used a similar exercise: assessing participants' decision making across four business situations of varying levels of uncertainty. In many of their responses, our growth leaders sounded a lot like entrepreneurs. In the scenarios with high levels of uncertainty, they focused on creating markets instead of trying to predict them. Rather than researching the ideal target market for a computer device, for instance, they indicated that they would use their existing relationships to help create a market.

In-depth analysis of our quantitative evaluations also found that out Catalysts were more flexible in their use of shaping efforts and prediction than either traditional managers or expert entrepreneurs. They were more flexible than expert entrepreneurs in their use of prediction, intensely avoiding it in the scenarios that were unpredictable, but increasing their use of predictive tools (NPV, market research, and the like) in the more predictable scenarios. We believe that this flexibility may explain Catalysts' ability to think like entrepreneurs but still operate effectively in large organizations.

If you are like most managers who have grown up in mature organizations, you have been taught to be a predictor. You've learned to set very specific plans and goals, based on some estimate of what the future is likely to look like. You spend a lot of time trying to analyze that future in detail, hoping to figure out where the puck is headed. This is a great strategy when the world you're operating in is stable, but any prediction is only as good as the underlying data used to make it. Trouble is, you'll use predictions to plan your behavior even when the odds that your predictions will turn out to be accurate aren't very high.

Expert entrepreneurs act in pretty much the opposite way. They tend to be *shapers*. They don't like spending time trying to analyze where the future is headed. And even though their preferences are almost opposite those of traditional managers, they are just as unilateral in their behavior. Even when they've got good information that would facilitate accurate predicting, they tend to ignore it. They prefer shaping, regardless of whether the environment is stable or uncertain.

For managers pursuing growth projects in established companies, knowing when to employ traditional business approaches and when to think like an entrepreneur is a crucial skill. Adopting entrepreneurial thinking may be the best way to discover and pursue innovative growth opportunities, but using prediction tools may be necessary for establishing credibility and persuading a company's leaders to let you go after those opportunities your own way. The Catalysts stand out because they are much more flexible in their approach than either corporate managers or entrepreneurs—they make creative use of the best of both worlds. Where there are opportunities to predict, they predict, using tools like market forecasts and experts' assessments. Where there are opportunities to shape, they shape. The bottom line here is that growth leaders are willing to shift their approach to suit the circumstances.

Because prediction is used so extensively in large organizations, we spend a lot of time attempting it, even when it is not the best approach. When we assume that the future is outside of our control and spend our energy trying to analyze what it will look like, we miss opportunities to act in ways that influence the way the future actually develops. Unlike most managers, the Catalysts employ a set of shaping tools that help them uncover and pursue opportunities to grow a business from within large organizations. Like entrepreneurs, they use risk-minimizing tactics such as obtaining precommitments from customers—to the point where they often don't see their initiatives as very risky at all. And they are, in fact, much less risky than the triple-threat approaches we talked about in chapter 1—the ones that seek only needle movers, involve building new capabilities and resources, and exist in isolation from customers and partners.

Jim Steiner's story is a great example of shaping tactics at work in a large organization: First, Steiner got off to a running start, leveraging the resources, assets, and capabilities at his disposal. He began by taking an inventory of what existed throughout Corning—such as the skills and equipment for sealing glass to metal, metal plating, and glass coating, and the relationship with the production partner in China—and then he worked from there.

Second, he interacted with a customer, TI, and other partners very early on to shape the future rather than react to it. He created value for all parties by both influencing partners and being influenced *by* them. In particular, Steiner raised the bar on his customer. Rather than try to predict what people at TI would or wouldn't buy, and what they would be willing to pay, he asked them to make volume and price commitments beforehand. They said yes.

Finally, by following the first two tactics, Steiner worked his way into an opportunity using the least expensive options, such as using equipment and employees from other Corning divisions instead of buying new equipment and making new hires, and working with the partner in China instead of building a new factory. Instead of investing at a level that needed to be justified using traditional return-on-investment measures, he ended up risking only what he could afford to lose, an approach entrepreneurship researchers call "affordable loss investing."

Compare these three tactics with the traditional corporate process, which involves predictions of what the market will look like, detailed research to support those predictions, and cash flow forecasts to justify large investments in the opportunity so that you can go it alone and produce something (eventually) to show potential customers. The Catalysts take an alternative path. They escape the tyranny of organizations' fondness for prediction and analysis. They are willing to be risk takers, but never risk makers.

Jim Steiner was more about action in the marketplace than analysis in the boardroom. Sure, he did his homework—but then he *left the building*, finding partners to work with in the real world. He stopped calculating and started doing. Before we delve into the details of his and other Catalysts' practices, let's step back and look at why taking action is so important.

THE MAGIC OF ACTION

Long before Nike came up with the slogan "Just do it," the German author Goethe, in his epic *Faust*, described the power of escaping "analysis paralysis":

> Then indecision brings its own delays,
> And days are lost lamenting over lost days.
> Are you in earnest? Seize this very minute;
> What you can do, or dream you can do, begin it;
> Boldness has genius, power and magic in it.

We don't know if leaders like Jim Steiner read *Faust,* but we do know that he and the other Catalysts agree with Goethe. All exhibit the intense bias for action that we talked about in chapter 2. They inevitably choose *doing* over *analyzing*. For them, leading growth is not about forming committees and writing PowerPoints and sitting in boardrooms; it is about mucking around with ideas, making and selling things that customers want, and adapting through their feedback to make it work. Conrad Hall of Trader Publications, whom we'll get to know in chapter 5, said it clearly: "Our bias is, if it's a good idea, let's *try* it. Let's not invest a fortune in market research, which many times gives you the wrong answer anyway. Let's launch the thing and let the market tell us whether it's a good idea or a bad idea."

Corporate bureaucracies all too often create analytical couch potatoes, loath to put down the Doritos and get moving. As Discovery Channel's Dawn McCall pointed out:

> It's like when you're sitting on the couch and some-
> body says, "Well, let's go do something." The biggest

challenge is just getting up. You can have all the facts and figures in the world, but until you flip that switch and say, "OK, I've got enough. Here's where we're going," nothing happens. And I think a lot of people just get mired in the place of "let me just look at one more thing before I make that decision." But no matter how long you take, you're never going to know everything.

The ratio of what you *know* to what you *don't know* is fundamentally different when you are growing a business than it is when you are managing what already exists. If, in pursuit of growth, you wait until you know as much as you do about an existing business, you won't get anywhere. Often even bothering to try to get such numbers, using traditional market research, is not something the Catalysts consider worthwhile. John Haugh of Mars/Masterfoods (we told his story in chapter 2) explained his view:

> We didn't know what the right answer was, but we also knew that doing another twelve months of research wasn't going to get us any better answers. Because in the end, you have got to take this thing out and test-drive it, and see if it works. Most new products fail— most fail despite the fact that the research is always done. And it's done by really, really smart people. The best way to get there is to put more ideas in the market. At least *try*. As Wayne Gretzky says, you miss one hundred percent of the shots you never take. So at least start shooting.

By taking action early on, the Catalysts:

1. Win validation for their ideas from outside "experts" and thereby create momentum for the new idea
2. Demonstrate their ability to deliver on their promises

3. Produce *real* data that help them improve the value proposition

Let's look at each of these in more detail.

Validation from influential outsiders—often customers, distributors, or partners in adjacent industries—silences internal critics by changing the focus from theoretical debates in conference rooms to early results in the marketplace. Walgreens's willingness to give Jeff Semenchuk from Pfizer a few shelves in a few stores to try out a line of portable health-care products made it tough for the professional doubters at Pfizer to derail the initiative's progress. This kind of outside support can shift the balance of power from internal naysayers to the leaders of growth, and the question from "Why?" to "Why not?" For entrepreneurial thinkers in large, established organizations, battling the naysayers is one of the most difficult and time-consuming challenges. Think back to the fixed-mindset folks we described in chapter 2, who are more comfortable avoiding new experiences than seeking them out and always want the comfort of certainty. They are the guardians of the status quo. Staying in the conference room yields them home field advantage.

Sometimes the outsiders whom growth leaders enlist to their cause are potential partners in adjacent industries; sometimes they are supply chain partners. Best of all are outsiders who are actual customers. As one of our leaders observed: "The day you convince your customer and he starts marketing for you, then you've won." Recall how TI's commitment to purchase a certain amount of volume from Corning helped accelerate revenue growth in Steiner's division.

The Catalysts use early action and the tangible success

it spawns to create a sense of urgency and build momentum for their initiatives. Rather than expending their energy trying to *push* new initiatives through the often reluctant organization, they engage outsiders to help *pull* the initiatives out of it.

Early actions are also powerful devices for building credibility by demonstrating the ability to execute. At NBC, when John Wallace needed to find resources to pursue his growth goal of opening up new media channels for existing content at the network, he did so by centralizing production and distribution. But he didn't ask key internal clients like the *Today* show staff to just rely on his *promise* that the new centralized approach wouldn't interfere with the quality and timeliness of their work. He designed a rigorous and thorough process of testing and iteration that involved them every step of the way. "We don't just say, 'Trust us and we'll get back to you in six months when everything's built,'" he explained.

Equally important, early actions often generate information that dramatically improves the new value proposition. Rich Combs of Power Distribution Inc. (PDI), a leading provider of power distribution equipment for large data management facilities and "server farms," described why he and his team chose certain customers to test out early versions of any design: because "they find things wrong that we would never find." Consider, for example, the company's initial designs for remote power devices (two-foot-by-eight-foot towers, each containing four panels). When parts shifted during the first shipment and couldn't be adjusted, Combs and his team immediately responded by designing an adjustable model. Customers of *that* model then reported that they needed better access to the bottoms and sides of the panels. Again, the team responded quickly with a new design. Subsequent customers asked for yet another enhancement (neutral switching), which PDI incorporated into the next version. Action, Combs told us, is an essential element of the design process. "You can sit there and design something toward one hundred percent right—in this business you tend to do that—but you'll never be one hundred percent right until it gets out in the field."

The Catalysts get out into the market and test their new business ideas using a set of risk-minimizing, learning-maximizing moves tailored to the demands of an uncertain world. Let's examine in depth the tactics they use.

Tactic 1: The Catalysts Get a Running Start

Rather than first identify specific goals and then try to acquire the capabilities and resources necessary to reach them, Catalysts let the assets and capabilities at their disposal lead the way. This doesn't mean that they have no goals—they just don't lock into specific ones early on in ways that reduce their ability to follow the opportunities that arise as the business develops. As Steiner's experience illustrates, Corning's *means* determined in large part the opportunities he and his team pursued. Indeed, they had decided at the outset to consider only possibilities that would call on their established technologies and contacts. TI's proposed opportunity met that criterion.

At Pfizer, Jeff Semenchuk's line of portable health-care products, called Mosaic, was based on the company's existing brands such as Listerine, Sudafed, and Benadryl. Instead of developing entirely new products, the company found new ways to present the familiar ones, packaging them to be portable and discreet—a concept that could be applied to many brands. Semenchuk also got a running start with the new offering by working with retailers that already carried Pfizer products, convincing them to devote just a bit of shelf space to test the new line.

Starting with what was at hand even extends into customer selection; Catalysts often target their growth initiatives to their existing customers. Tim Peters at Dell sold printers online to the people who were already buying Dell computers. John Wallace of NBC redirected existing video content into new digital channels (like cell phones) that his customers were migrating toward. Stephen Oswald at Sullair, an industrial air compressor manufacturer, bundled a more complete set of products and services to sell to the customers that already bought Sullair's compressed air products. The Catalysts leverage their organizations, taking advantage of the fact that they already have much of what they need. And they already have customers.

For Sanjiv Yajnik at Capital One, building on the company's means was a priority with specific benefits: "We leverage our organization—we leverage existing capabilities to the hilt. It just pays back massively in low cost and high commitment in the future."

Speed is another benefit. Building new systems, establishing new customer relationships, opening new facilities, and getting buy-in from Corporate are all long and involved processes. For the Catalysts, time is often in as short supply as money. By using existing resources and capabilities, the break-even point of their efforts is dramatically lower and so they get there faster (a point we'll talk a lot more about in chapter 7). Working with what is at hand gives the Catalysts a running start.

How do the Catalysts effectively redeploy people, facilities, equipment, and know-how into a new high-growth opportunity?

- They take an inventory of assets and capabilities.
- They find talent across organizational boundaries.
- They draw on external resources as needed.

In the search for growth, the Catalysts look around at the assets and capabilities at hand and then gravitate toward those that are underutilized. John Zahurancik looked at giant power supplier AES's chief asset—its infrastructure of power lines—and figured out how to use it to deliver broadband as well as electricity. Clay Presley started with school notebooks, one of Carolina Pad's biggest product categories, and then found a way to recast them as something other than a commodity.

But they don't limit themselves to their own slice of the corporation—they look across organizational boundaries. Steiner saw possibilities across Corning. At Raytheon, Michael Booen assembled existing technology and capabilities from across the company to produce Vigilant Eagle—a value breakthrough that ensured commercial air safety by protecting *airports* rather than individual aircraft.

Working across organizational boundaries isn't easy, but it is essential to increasing the leaders' bandwidth without making additional investments. In big corporations, it is hard to know what and where skill sets exist. An identified growth opportunity provides a concrete frame of reference that helps identify precisely what you need to learn. The growth leaders built internal and external networks of relationships that helped them figure all that out when a growth possibility materialized—and helped them evaluate and pursue the opportunity.

But the Catalysts aren't just out making new friends. They are deliberate about understanding other people's expertise, their passions, and the resources to which they are connected. Catalysts like Michael Booen don't go up and down the chain of command to ask permission to engage talented employees from other divisions; they rely on their personal contacts and the lure of a great project and go directly to the right people inside or outside the company. This increases their reach to resources exponentially, allowing them to pull in talented partners with important skills that they lack. Clay Presley at Carolina Pad needed a young designer in touch with preteen and teenage girls to realize his vision of a fashion notebook. He already knew where to find one, having worked with Jacqueline McFee (we'll hear more about her and Presley in chapter 4) in a previous job.

In this process of connecting to a broad set of resources and capabilities, the Catalysts regularly entertain a simple question: "What else can I do with this stuff?" While that may sound too open-ended, tossing this question around with customers and partners leads to a relatively short list of intriguing possibilities. And by employing the next two tactics, they can move from intriguing possibilities to genuine opportunities.

Tactic 2: The Catalysts Win Early Yeses

The Catalysts, like most entrepreneurs pursuing a new venture, face many questions about how to proceed. What exactly should the offering involve? How will they produce it? Who will want to buy it? How will they sell it? The

Catalysts resolve those uncertainties by persuading others to work with them (that's where the early yeses come in) to create mutually advantageous solutions.

Before we examine early yeses, let's again compare the entrepreneurial approach of shaping the future with its alternative—predicting where a market is going and positioning an offering within that predicted market. In prediction mode, managers take the "market" they predict will materialize as a given: The trick is to stake out the best parts of it. Catalysts don't assume *anything* about the market that they don't have to. Instead, they work with real customers in ways that allow the specifics of the final value proposition to *emerge*. They don't impose their view of the future on those around them. Instead, they work with others in a process of *co-creation* in which they are both influencing and open to being influenced.

Is the world a result of your efforts? Or is the world outside of your control? As we saw in chapter 2, the Catalysts would answer yes to the first question and no to the second. Their belief in the ability to shape the future is part of their wiring—it is part of their basic creed.

The Catalysts' shaping efforts center on engagement with customers and partners. In essence, they are able to work around forecasts and predictions, because direct involvement with others gives them much more specific and useful information. Traditional marketing efforts often begin with broad market pictures, characterizations of various players and segments. The Catalysts turn that around: Markets and market segments emerge over time as a result of specific interactions among specific people. These interactions, which often occur early on and involve outsiders, help them think through what the opportunity might actually be.

Chuck Culbertson, a government contractor at Schafer, provides a fascinating example of how interaction and co-operation can broaden existing capability sets—without additional investment—and create significant growth. When Culbertson took over the engineering consulting group at Schafer, the firm was a distant fourth or fifth in the market. Industry leader Booz Allen towered over com-petitors. Culbertson's challenge was to figure out how his relatively small firm could win major contracts. Without any major investment or change in the marketplace, Cul-bertson turned Schafer's size—seemingly a strategic liability—into a strategic asset. He leveraged the company's position as a nonthreatening peer to create Team Schafer, a virtual network of small firms, all former rivals. Customers loved this new value proposition, which allowed them to staff each new project with a handpicked team of the most suitable talent available from among the members of Team Schafer. Soon, Schafer had moved up to second position in the industry.

The *supply* of talent, versus the demand for it, became Culbertson's new problem. Again, his recruiting approach was creative and collaborative. Rather than rush out and hire more full-time Schafer employees on the basis of pre-dicted needs, he reached out to new talent by establishing a virtual network of prequalified potential employees. "I build an active inventory of prospective employees. We call them periodically and remind them that Schafer's still interested in them. If I can then find a client to buy their services, I can hire them. And two weeks later, they're on-site. So we're letting someone else carry our inventory, if you will."

Like Culbertson's alliance-building through Team Schafer, finding outsider partners helps the Catalysts shape the specifics of their opportunity. Partners commit to working together to develop the opportunity, share risk, and generate valuable insights. Rather than viewing these partners as potential competitors, growth leaders design the opportunity to be a solid win for both parties.

This kind of mutual development and delivery of the business concept bumps up against one of the most cherished beliefs in the strategy realm: that the ability to capture value is a function of your success at keeping a secret. The rise of networks and the attendant recognition of their power—along with the increasing difficulty of keeping anything secret for long—has shattered that belief. One of the most myth-busting business models of our time is that of the computer operating system Linux. The success of the Linux model—the system's code can be altered and redistributed by any user— illustrates the tremendous power unleashed by engaging customers in the ongoing development of the offering, especially in the debugging process. "No bug can resist a million eyeballs" is how open-source-software enthusi- ast Eric Raymond described the outcome produced by "releasing early and often" to customers and collaborators.*

But all partners are not created equal, and the right ones are not always obvious. Wasting time on the wrong ones can be lethal. The Catalysts have an amazingly sim- ple way to separate the wheat from the chaff, the right partner from their evil twin: It is getting an early yes.

An early yes provides the market test for a running start. The idea is painfully straightforward and is violated at substantial risk: Potential customers lead only to potential

---

* Eric S. Raymond, *The Cathedral and the Bazaar: Musings on Linux and Open Source by an Accidental Revolutionary* (O'Reilly, 1999).

markets. As the Catalysts work through decisions about how to develop the new opportunity, they consider first and foremost whether they can win yeses from important stakeholders. A yes is the difference between a potential customer and a real customer, between a committed partner and an interested one.

Yes, I will give you shelf space in my store to try that. Yes, I will place an order. Yes, I will send over two engineers to work on that project. Yes, I will share the development cost on that software. Yes, I will prepay for the order. There exists an almost infinite set of valuable yeses to new opportunities. But they all have one thing in common: a material commitment from the person saying yes. They are a tangible representation of their intent to co-create the future; they are the opposite of making decisions on the basis of predictions.

Jeff Semenchuk relied on an early yes. To bring Pfizer's portable health-care concept to fruition, he knew that he needed to involve retailers early on. Would they be interested in selling and distributing the new line? Offering theoretical arguments to retailers and Pfizer's own brand managers about the viability of this new category would never get the initiative off the ground. Semenchuk believed in the potential of portable health-care products, but he had to get into the market to support his intuition with data. Walgreens, one of the largest drug store chains in the United States, provided his yes by devoting a few shelves in a few stores to the new product. This early yes allowed him to answer questions that he couldn't answer otherwise, start the marketing process, and accelerate efforts to convince others within the company that the opportunity was more than a pipe dream.

Despite their rich repertoires, the Catalysts did not rely solely on their own instincts. Their focus on winning a yes required them to listen to their partners and work with them to refine the offering.

John Haugh, leading Mars's effort to grow the luxury chocolate business Ethel M, took this to heart: "One of the things that I think we've done pretty effectively is to go to our partners (in one instance to the company developing the packaging) and say, 'All right, we're in this together. If it works, you're going to sell us a whole bunch of boxes. Therefore, what's your skin in the game? Help us develop a box that's unique; help us develop a box that we can afford.'"

Demanding an early yes provides a reality check on customers and partners. Importantly, looking for an early yes minimizes the influence of *potential* customers. Potential customers are a false positive: They act like customers, they look like customers, but they may not be actual customers. We use the word *potential* in a pejorative sense here. Potential customers may lead you down a primrose path that involves investment on your part, with only the promise of future business that may or may not materialize. To weed these out, the Catalysts place some demands on those who have the privilege of influencing the growth opportunity. They want to influence and be influenced only by *actual* customers and *actual* partners.

An early yes also provides direct evidence of the value of the opportunity. Without this validation, growth leaders struggle to convince organizational skeptics of the potential of their projects. Predictions about what customers want or where markets are heading are rarely perfect:

They make an easy target for skeptics. Early yeses provide traction—the concrete evidence of actual markets that growth leaders need.

Those who have tried to capture a growth opportunity in a big company without this kind of traction can attest to the difficulty. Those who seek new opportunities without an early yes and with little information to justify detailed profit predictions face an uphill battle. Without real evidence, the organization is left to make decisions the only ways it knows how: on gut feel (which most corporations try to avoid) or using detailed financial models that forecast market size and share, and predict the profitability of the opportunity over the near to medium term (we'll talk more about this in chapter 5). The yes that Jim Steiner was able to get from Texas Instruments, a hard order for the product on the basis of a couple of prototypes, moved the organization beyond those analyses and into action.

How can *you* achieve an early yes? By letting relationships with outsiders influence your ideas and by raising the bar on customers. As Catalysts rise up in their organizations, they stay connected to the outside. Don't delegate all of the opportunities to work with important outside organizations. Interesting people and organizations that are willing to be honest help refine your entrepreneurial thinking. Growth leadership requires connecting new ideas and possibilities to outsiders who can improve those ideas. Have one meeting a week with someone outside your organization—aimed at simply keeping in touch, exploring what you're each working on, and determining how you can help each other. When you come across a specific opportunity, these contacts will likely be interested and available to provide useful feedback.

The Catalysts raised the bar on continued cooperation. Ask for commitments in a broad sense, test to see whether the people you are working with are more than just potential partners, and require some tangible representation of their desire to shape the future with you.

By taking on the market to get a yes—instead of fighting internal battles in conference rooms with hypothetical data—you'll be letting outside partners do your work for you.

Tactic 3: The Catalysts Manage Affordable Loss Rather Than Return on Investment

Capital expenditures are a big deal; bigger capital expenditures are a bigger deal. Capital expenditures to enter uncharted waters—uncertain new markets and lines of business—may be the biggest deal of all. By thinking in terms of what they are willing to lose, instead of desperately needing to win, the Catalysts greatly minimize the risk of their projects. You'd think they were spending their own money.

For the Catalysts, affordable loss investing is getting into the market, and getting to an early yes, as cheaply as possible. In most cases where they can't win an early yes with an amount of money that is under their control— and that keeps their projects below the corporate radar— they redesign the opportunity rather than move up the hierarchy looking for more money. In this way, they not only think like entrepreneurs but also spend money like them (or rather, *don't* spend money like them).

The Catalysts stay within affordable loss in creative ways. Moving dollars around inside their budgets, staying below signature authority, and using executive sponsorship for small discretionary expenditures are the most common approaches. The key is to keep the investment small enough that the intrigue of the opportunity grossly outweighs the losses if it doesn't work out. The Catalysts focus on determining the dollar amount that people will spend to prove them wrong—because they *just might be right.*

Conrad Hall at Trader built out the company's employment publications on the affordable loss approach. "Our start-ups have typically been done at very, very low levels of investment, low levels of operating losses for short periods of time, and then they go into the profit side of the equation." Typically they'd drop one person into a market, get neck deep in the effort, and make a larger commitment only if the initiative connected to the company's core skills and if they had an early yes. All this would happen quickly enough to recoup their affordable loss expenses in short order.

Jim Steiner at Corning didn't have to justify his investments in exploring the opportunity to move up the value chain in the DLP business. Visiting with customers at a trade conference was affordable. This led to an invitation. Supporting the engineering conversations that led to some prototypes was affordable. The prototypes led to a commitment from Texas Instruments. That commitment itself dramatically raised the level of what was affordable because it virtually eliminated the risk in manufacturing the early orders. If the conversations and prototypes had led to nothing, no harm would have been done. Making affordable investments enabled the effort to operate under the radar and kept Steiner's team flexible if it needed to adapt to a no or a "not yet" from Texas Instruments.

This leads us to the two key benefits of the affordable loss approach. First, it maintains flexibility. Because they are not locked into a plan, the Catalysts can explore different ways to solve the challenges they face. They are in a position to respond to feedback and surprises from the marketplace rather than ignore or deny them.

Second, consider the o0pposite of affordable loss investing. Is it possible to slow down innovation by giving managers too much money? We believe that it is. A surfeit of cash discourages managers from finding partners and chasing early yeses. It gives them the luxury of *not* connecting directly to customers early on to find and test opportunities. They can procrastinate. Imagine if a customer says, "Hey, I like what you're doing, but can you change it just a bit? Can you work with us differently?" A team with a lot of cash is significantly less likely to jump at the opportunity. Affordable loss investing reinforces strong connections to *actual* rather than *potential* markets. The reality is that entrepreneurs *are* usually playing with their own money. That gives them some powerful advantages.

To summarize:

One of the keys to the kingdom of creating significant revenue growth is to help corporate managers learn how and when to think the way entrepreneurs do—to gain the best of both worlds.

Entrepreneurial thinking is more than just a fresh take on uncertainty; it's a willingness to act in the face of it. By starting with one customer who will become a partner in creating a broader market and by leveraging internal resources, entrepreneurs and growth leaders respond to undefined products and markets by taking decisive action. Like much of what we've got to say in this book, it's not rocket science—it's more like common sense. But that doesn't mean it's a common approach in large organizations. Therein lies the opportunity.

ENTER THE ENTREPRENEUR

Now it's time for *you* to put down the Doritos and get off the couch. Start by assessing whether the tactics that you use are focused more on shaping or on predicting, using the chart below:

	TACTICS FOR SHAPING	TACTICS FOR PREDICTION
Where to Start	Start with what you have and see where it takes you.	Collect data, analyze, make predictions, and select a goal.
Measuring Risks and Returns	Determine what you can afford to lose.	Calculate your expected return.
Attitude Toward Outsiders	Seek out partners with whom you can create win-win solutions.	Keep it proprietary whenever you can— go it alone.
Dealing with Change	Stay open to opportunity and exploit changes.	Avoid surprises.
Approach	Be willing to learn as you go.	Create a plan and do whatever you have to to stick to it.

Here are some further questions to guide your efforts to develop your entrepreneurial thinking as you work to catalyze organic growth:

1. What specific resources, capabilities, and relationships can you identify and access throughout your organization—and across a broader network of relationships? Work to understand how else they might be used. Specifically develop a new relationship with at least one person outside but related to your firm, or inside your firm but in a different group.

2. What possibilities for new business models, customer interaction, and applications of those resources seem to excite you and the people in your network? Begin to design how else you can work with those resources to create a future that you value.

3. Are there proactive ways to resolve uncertainty facing the people and organizations with whom and with which you work? Don't worry about whether they are feasible yet. Dream of the possible ways you could work together to build a "world" where that uncertainty is overcome.

4. What three yeses do you need to win in order to have real validation of your opportunity? Who do you believe could guarantee the success of your next steps? Get in the mix; be persuasive and be flexible.

5. What resources and commitments from specific potential customers and partners would indicate to you that they had genuine passion to create an actual rather than a potential market? As you get deeper into your opportunities, raise the bar.

6. How much can you afford to lose to win those initial yeses? Estimate what you think it will take to get those three yeses you've identified, prioritize them, and ask

yourself, "If I am completely wrong, and lose this money trying to get that yes, will that be okay? Will I have learned something important about this opportunity?"

7. Given a specific level of affordable loss, what yeses can you realistically win for that dollar amount? Recalibrate. Oftentimes you can win those yeses for free, or maybe the cost of a plane ticket or an extra day at a conference. You don't need to invest and develop the operational system before you can chase early yeses.

4

IT'S ALREADY THERE—
REFRAME TO FIND IT

_____

What allows the Catalysts to act differently is that they see differently first. By doing so, they discover ways to create value for their customers without relying on the development of dramatic new products or technology breakthroughs. Instead, they use their repertoires and entrepreneurial ways of thinking to find opportunities that are already there but overlooked by competitors. They practice "Cynthia-centricity" (more about her later), looking beyond sterile marketing segmentations to understand the details of their customers' lives. In this chapter, we'll look at the power of escaping industry mental models and reframing—looking through a different lens.

Clay Presley, like most people, did not want to be in a commodity business. The years he spent as a CPA at a major auditing firm convinced him that he never wanted to compete on price. But a commodity business was exactly where he found himself in the spring of 2000, when he took on the challenge of leading Carolina Pad & Paper. The paper company, like others in the piney woods of North Carolina, seemed stuck in the past, mired in a mentality that measured success in terms of selling "paper by the pound" and filling capacity in outdated manufacturing plants.

At Carolina Pad, the commodity product was school notebooks, sold to second-tier retailers to use as loss leaders. Presley soon saw that Carolina Pad couldn't turn around its dismal sales and profits by sticking with this business model. Finding the solution would require looking at the business through a completely different lens. Maybe school notebooks didn't have to be aimed at a mass market. Maybe there were consumers out there who would be willing, even eager, to buy a notebook designed specifically for them—and to pay a premium price for the privilege.

Presley's success at Carolina Pad demonstrates the power of *reframing*: seeing things differently and then, as a result, *acting* differently. Reframing uncovers opportunities that are already there but are often obscured by accepted sets of industry or company beliefs about what is possible or promising. Each Catalyst uses reframing as an essential tool for tapping into new possibilities for revenue growth, but Presley's story is especially powerful because it is hard to imagine a business that seems a less likely candidate for organic growth.

When Presley landed at Carolina Pad, the company was in financial distress. Not only were margins low, so was volume. The way out of this hole wasn't immediately clear. Carolina Pad was already very lean, with little left to trim on the expense side. Moreover, it couldn't afford to replace its obsolete manufacturing equipment.

But Presley arrived with a few secrets up his sleeve. He wasn't a traditional "paper guy," nor was he your average CPA. He'd taken a job with a Big Eight firm out of college mainly because he was promised that his first stint would be in Saudi Arabia. This proved to be an interesting move for a young man who had never been out of the United

States. Seven years of auditing all types of businesses had equipped him with the kind of broad repertoire discussed in chapter 2. In particular, Presley was able to spot a good (or bad) business model at twenty paces. After leaving public accounting, he worked in a family stationery business, so he knew that the paper business had possibilities; it wasn't all commodity hell. He'd reached the point in his career of wanting to own his firm. Carolina Pad's owner was not only looking for help but was willing to trade equity to get it. It seemed like the perfect match: a leader who saw some new possibilities and a business desperate for better results.

In the face of these sobering realities, Presley and his team adopted an ambitious goal (Jim Collins might even call it big, hairy, and audacious)*: "We wanted to be good at something, and we wanted to develop a reputation as being the go-to person, the go-to company, for whatever product we came out with." Presley's hunch, based on his experiences in the stationery business and Carolina Pad's unsuccessful past efforts, was that integrating fashion into the back-to-school arena was the place to start. School notebooks, long the company's bread-and-butter product, didn't have to be humdrum, he believed; they could be turned into a fashion statement. The target market was obvious to the team: preteen and teenage girls, who—market research told them—had abundant spending money that they would happily part with for trendy products. The equation also worked for their immediate customers— retail buyers—who were excited at the prospect of selling moneymakers instead of loss leaders.

---

* James C. Collins and Jerry I. Porras, *Built to Last: Successful Habits of Visionary Companies* (HarperCollins, 1997).

Having decided to pursue this fundamental reframing of the company's value proposition from commodity supplier to purveyor of cool, Presley and his team faced a number of major obstacles, not the least of which was the idea of a group of middle-aged men designing notebooks for young girls. "We laughed about that all the time," Presley recalled. Fortunately, they had the sense not even to try. Enter Jacqueline McFee, a twenty-something design consultant whom Presley had worked with previously. She had her pulse on the trends in the teenage market and a flair for selling the old guys on the wisdom of her ideas. "You want to believe everything she says," Presley told us. "She was our springboard into the new venture." Close enough in age to the target market, McFee modeled the customer for them, helped the team visualize the possibilities, and soon got them all on board.

More challenging was Carolina Pad's inability to manufacture the high-end notebooks in its outdated plants. To overcome this obstacle, Presley made the tough call, telling the team to "go develop product that we can sell. Don't worry about developing product that we can manufacture." Eventually, the company outsourced the manufacturing of the new notebooks to China.

Although most of Presley's senior management team readily embraced the new approach to their business, many on the company's sales force were less enthusiastic. Presley explained: "We called them the OPGs, the old paper guys. Old paper guys love to buy a pound of paper for 25 cents, convert it, and sell it for 32 cents—that made them happy. . . . We weren't going to get anywhere with them on this fashion product." Many on the sales force needed to go in order to create a group ready to sell the idea to major customers. "I've learned that you can't be afraid to change," Presley observed. "You've got to change and change quickly—not callously, but quickly—and make sure that you get the right people in the right place."

Finally, an important aspect of Presley's reframing process, one that generated a new set of elements to play with in order to achieve success, was an intense focus on creating a compelling value proposition for chain-store buyers. Presley took a different look not only at his world of school notebooks but also at his buyers' world. He knew that he needed to create a story about the new product that would make sense to the buyers and that would win them over. Presley thought about the reward systems at his buyers' firms, which rarely valued buying loss leaders:

> We knew that our buyers at the retailers were incurring the loss, but they weren't getting any benefit or any credit for the market basket that was being put together for the whole store. . . . So we started looking at notebooks, saying if we could provide them with a product that would allow *their* customers, the end customers, to step up in price and allow the retailer to make more money on it, then our buyers are going to look like heroes, and we're going to look like heroes because we're all making more money on this particular product.

Attention to buyers as customers and this deeper understanding of their needs paid off handsomely for Carolina Pad. Wal-Mart, in particular, played a pivotal role in the development of the new business, opting to carry one of the first four fashion notebooks Carolina Pad produced and providing the early yes that we talked about in chapter 3. Psychologically, signing up Wal-Mart—even before a single notebook sold at retail—was a powerful event. It strengthened the story that salesmen told other potential customers. The willingness of the world's largest retailer to carry the product was reassuring both inside and outside the firm. As the new notebook began to sell briskly, Wal-Mart's sophisticated POS data demonstrated just how well it would perform. Both confidence and interest in the fashion notebook soared.

Presley emphasized the important role that close attention to retailers' (not just end consumers') needs played in the company's success story:

> In today's retail environment, clearly the buyers don't have the time to try and figure out a very creative plan that they can execute to generate more profitability for their particular departments. That's really part of *our* job. And we've embraced that to the point that we spend a lot of time and energy taking a program and dissecting it, whether it's including our products or a competitor's products, and trying to make recommendations to our buyers that make sense for them—not just for us, but for them. . . . At the end of the day, they'll view us as being an asset—bringing something to the table every time we come in there.

The success of the reinvented company, now called CPP International, continues. Deepened relationships with top retailers spawn an ever-increasing array of opportunities. Its competitors, you ask? Still mired in the "old paper guy" mentality and struggling to fill obsolete plants, they have been slow to emulate CPP's approach.

Presley attributes his ongoing success, in part, to the inclusiveness of the conversations at CPP. "Our goal is to continue to grow this company at a reasonably aggressive rate, realizing that we're in a very mature industry," he explains. "My basic premise is that I treat everybody the way

I want to be treated so anybody has an opportunity to put ideas on the table. We're a creative environment: People can bring their idea to the table, and if it makes sense and fits in with our strategy, then we execute it. It doesn't matter where the idea comes from."

"I think you have to constantly reinvent yourself," he continues. "We have had so many changes in this organization that you create an atmosphere that change is the norm. That's very, very important, especially in a company that's in a mature market."

Just five years after Presley launched the redesigned notebooks, revenues and profits have doubled, and CPP has accomplished a goal that once seemed impossible: achieving distribution through the top two retailers in each major category—chain store, drugstore, and office supply superstore. Now viewed by retailers as an innovative sales and marketing company rather than a stodgy commodity paper supplier, CPP demonstrates the power of reframing— of finding new opportunities by looking through a different lens at a reality that competitors don't see and creating new value propositions with that insight. Reframing is where Catalysts light the fuse that can ignite an explosion of growth. They bring together who they are and where they've been, and combine that with a deeper understanding of who their customers are and where they want to go. As we noted earlier, the biggest obstacle to growth is not in the marketplace but in the minds of managers.

It all sounds pretty obvious when listening to Presley's story after the fact. We bet, though, that it doesn't look that obvious as you stand in your business today and look forward. Let's unpack how the Catalysts found their new lens.

CATALYSTS LOOK INSIDE OUT *AND* OUTSIDE IN

When it comes to seeing differently, it is easy to get in your own way. With all of the buzz about "innovation" and "breakthrough thinking," we think that we have to come up with wildly creative ideas to grow a business successfully. We're told that we need to "get out of our box." But our box is the sum of our experiences; it's what makes managers valuable. As we said in chapter 2, you *are* your box.

The Catalysts first make sure that they have built bigger boxes—then they *use* their boxes instead of trying to escape from them. They use all of the experiences in their repertoires. At the same time, they work hard to climb into customers' boxes along with them—to look at the world through their eyes. Practicing the kind of *seeing* that allows them to find more powerful value propositions is not rocket science, nor is it black magic. Like Clay Presley's notebook idea, what they come up with may often look obvious in retrospect. They just work at looking *inside out* and *outside in* simultaneously.

Making Your Box Work for You

To look inside out, you begin with yourself. Your personality, ways of thinking, and personal repertoire shape how you think and what you do. Those elements become part of the "wiring" that we talked about in chapter 2. The Catalysts leveraged the contents of their individual boxes as the breeding ground for the particular growth initiatives they identified and pursued. Remember Mark O'Neill, the leader who runs Kelvingrove Museum in Scotland? Even in a world that values creativity as much as his does, O'Neill sees the emphasis on innovation as misplaced, arguing that many people confuse having good ideas with something called "creativity":

> Anything we've done that's innovative belongs far more to digging deep to understand what we're trying to do and how to do it better than it does to creativity. If you develop a deep understanding of the impact you're trying to make, that *will* produce innovation. But innovation is secondary.

"Cynthia-centricity"

At the same time that the Catalysts are experts at looking inside out, tapping into their accumulated experiences and making their boxes work for them, they are intensely focused outside themselves and their firms as well, always looking to deepen their knowledge of customers and partners. There is no phrase in business today more overused and underachieved than *customer focus.* But the *real* deal here—the one that moved the Catalysts beyond rhetoric to action—is being deeply interested in the *details of their customers' lives as people,* rather than as an impersonal collection of targets or categories. Our code word for this deep empathic customer focus is "Cynthia-centricity," an idea introduced to us by Jim Cass, a Mars/Masterfoods manager who told us that he was not "customer-centric"; he was "Cynthia-centric." He went on to describe Cynthia to us: She is a single mother with limited time and income who has gone to a lot of trouble to purchase personalized M&M's for her son's birthday party. Sadly, they arrive a day late, and Cass uses Cynthia's disappointment as a constant reminder of what it means to be a day late in his business.

The Catalysts emphasize this kind of deep focus on their customers, moving beyond merely responding to customers' requests to anticipating their desires, from giving customers what everyone thinks they need to giving them what they actually want. The Catalysts rarely make the mistake of assuming others think like they do. "Build it and they will come" is anathema to them. Mark O'Neill told us about a celebration a friend had recently held in his honor: "One of my closest friends organized a celebration, a lunch party. And the main course was shrimp. And I hate shellfish. And we do that so often. We give what is a treat for us as a treat for other people." Conrad Hall of Trader Publications argued that you need to start in the marketplace: "You either see an opportunity or you see a problem. But you're still starting off from the same initial 'let's look at what is going on.'" The search is for the need—what he called the "hole in the grid"—that no one else is paying attention to.

But even this "outside in" part is personal to them. When Jeff Immelt of GE first pronounced that "all growth is personal," we weren't sure what that meant. The Catalysts show just how true Immelt's insight is. Their interest in and experience with customers is intensely personal and direct. They don't like to rely on secondhand reports and market research studies. They know that segmentation classifications can just as easily obscure real customer needs as illuminate them. Their understanding of customers as *people* versus *categories,* an understanding often rooted in early career experiences in sales or service, is an essential part of the repertoire they bring to growth opportunities.

John Wallace of NBC believes that his previous jobs running a regional TV distribution network and managing the sales office of a Philadelphia affiliate gave him a lifelong advantage: "I think that I had a unique advantage that other leaders might not have had because of the fact that I had, from one of my first jobs, an understanding of the customer and of the need to listen." Even those leaders without significant sales experience spoke of customers as the core of their business, and of knowing them as an "investment" that could not be delegated. In making this investment, they were looking to learn not just about consumers' preferences and opinions, but more fundamentally about their *daily lives*. With this kind of insight, products and services exist in a context— the whole of the customer's experience—not the other way around. To these managers, customers were the "heroes" or the "boss," and we heard a lot of advice to "follow them home."

Customers, as the Catalysts described them, spanned the value chain, including adjacent buyers as well as those further down the chain. For both industrial and consumer products, the end user was always an important focus—but so was the retailer or distributor, as Clay Presley's story illustrates so powerfully. Learning about the customer was, for the Catalysts, less about conducting traditional market research and holding focus groups and more about using such direct methods as observation and similar empathic design approaches. It was more about *observing* than asking, and about identifying unarticulated needs rather than responding to requests for solutions. Kal Patel, who led leading electronics retailer Best Buy's conversion from what he called "product shifting" (moving products from manufacturers to end customers, with a focus on inventory management) to "customer-centricity," observed: "Take small businesses. These are customers that already come into our store every day. How do you serve them better? What new value propositions do you serve them with? To learn what they need, you have to go *deep down* into the store interaction and learn from that as opposed to some standard marketing research reports."

For the Catalysts, growth is not primarily about *products*—it is about *value propositions*. In looking outside in, they place customers and their definition of value at the center of their attention. They make a personal investment of their time in understanding customers' needs and desires, use this understanding to develop more powerful value propositions, and often collaborate early on with value chain partners to co-develop growth initiatives. They take information from outside and use it to look inside, both within themselves and within their organizations, for creative ways to reframe their offerings. New products and services are a part of the story, of course, but other aspects of the business model—how they interact with value chain partners to produce, market, and distribute their offerings—are often equally important.

In some cases, their firms already had the capabilities, mindsets, and relationships to make the new value propositions work, but often there were missing pieces— new skills and partnerships that needed developing, old ways of thinking that needed abandoning, challenges that needed surmounting. We'll look first at some of the specific kinds of reframing the Catalysts invoked, and then we'll consider the steps they took to accomplish them.

SEVEN FORMULAS FOR REFRAMING

The Catalysts take multiple approaches to reframing their value propositions. We have grouped them into seven categories representing a series of *FROM* ≫ *TO* formulas. Taken together, they offer a menu of options for all businesses interested in growing organically through the development of enhanced value propositions.

Formula 1: Diving Deep		
FROM		**TO**
Commodity product for a mass market	>>	Differentiated value proposition for a particular customer

Clay Presley at Carolina Pad used one of the most common reframing approaches, taking a commodity product (school notebooks) aimed at a mass market and transforming it into a differentiated value proposition (a fashion statement) targeted at a particular market segment, in this case preteen and teenage girls. We call this kind of reframing the "deep dive" because it requires digging below the surface of what may look like a market with undifferentiated needs to find groups of buyers willing to pay premium prices for tailored value propositions.

Kal Patel at Best Buy describes the realization—developed by sending senior executives out to spend time on the floor at their stores—that their customers were not a mass market looking for products like fax machines and DVD players, but were instead discrete groups of people (soccer moms or real estate agents, for instance), each with their own needs. This led, in turn, to a dramatic shift in management attention from managing product inventory on shelves to examining customer needs, a shift Patel credits as the foundation of the firm's successful organic growth.

Close observation of customer groups, as Patel describes, as well as some traditional market segmentation approaches, were the kinds of tools that helped facilitate this transition, which was driven by one strategic question: "How can we get inside the head of individual customers to offer them something they will value more than the commodity product?"

Formula 2: **Swimming for the Surface**

FROM   **TO**

Customized product   **>>**   Standardized value proposition
for a single customer   for a larger group of customers

If Clay Presley at Carolina Pad and Kal Patel at Best Buy took a deep dive to narrow their target market, Rich Combs of PDI swam in the opposite direction, broadening demand for what had been a customized product. The company's design skills allowed PDI to work closely with AOL, a longstanding customer, to find a superior solution to a prototypical problem: "power towers," designed to expand a data center's capacity, whose cabinetry got in the way of their function. New partnerships with distributors with expanded market reach allowed PDI to find many other customers with the same problem. The strategic question here is, "How do we identify and reach a category of like-minded customers with similar needs?"

Formula 3: **Swimming Sideways**

FROM		**TO**
Current product	**>>**	**Adjacent needs**

Some Catalysts swim neither up nor down but sideways, moving from one product in their value chain to focus on adjacent needs. Peter Karpas at Intuit tapped into the company's deep expertise at writing software to help consumers manage large amounts of data in complicated situations—a skill that made Quicken, which emphasizes general expense management, and TurboTax, a leading tax computation software package, leaders in their respective areas. He used this strategy to target a similar need in an adjacent area—developing software, called Quicken Medical Expense Manager, that manages medical deductibles. In launching Swiffer, the hugely successful floor-cleaning system, Craig Wynett at Procter & Gamble (P&G) moved from the industry's historic focus on the detergent and focused instead on the mop, the other indispensable element in a clean floor. Tim Peters, in the same vein, took Dell's direct computer product expertise to printers.

In each of these moves, the leaders leveraged the firm's existing brand name and relationships with customers, plus its infrastructure and capabilities, as a broader platform from which to expand into related areas. They did so, in part, by going back to the customer's core problem—whether it was a dirty floor, too much paperwork, or complex electronics—and asking, "How do we apply our expertise to problems *related* to the one our customers already trust us to solve?"

Formula 4: Bundling

FROM   TO

Stand-alone individual product   **>>**   Comprehensive multiproduct
                                          solutions

Some of the Catalysts took the sideways strategy a step further, bundling multiple offerings to deliver a comprehensive solution. Stephen Oswald at Sullair shifted the business from one that sold individual air compressor products to one that bridged products and aftermarket offerings to offer reliable, cost-effective compressed air guaranteed when customers needed it. His customers had been buying products but really wanted compressed air. At Pfizer, Jeff Semenchuk took a set of unconnected stand-alone existing products and gave consumers the opportunity to assemble a portable "medicine cabinet" for their car, briefcase, or desk drawer. Andrew Edelmann at Merrill Lynch brought together private bankers and financial analysts, all previously offering individual, competing financial products, to create customized portfolios of blended products for high-net-worth clients.

As leaders move toward multiproduct solutions, the ability to work quickly and seamlessly across business lines in real time becomes paramount to success. Whether it was bringing together groups of engineers, product managers, or financial analysts, the Catalysts made sure to present a single, integrated face to the customer that masked the inevitable differences in perspective and business approach. They asked, "What outcome is the customer trying to achieve, and how can we work together to help achieve it?" As these stories demonstrate, there is enormous organic growth potential in surmounting these differences. Few manage to do it, but the rewards are great for those who succeed. Semenchuk's portable medicine cabinet business, for instance, is estimated to have a market potential of $500 million plus—all incremental to current sales.

***Formula 5:* Finding White Space**

FROM   **TO**

**Stand-alone business-unit,   >>   White-space value propositions
capabilities**

Another path to organic growth—one related to bundling products—is bringing together multiple *capabilities* that allow the creation of a new product, one that falls into the "white space" between divisions of a company. It is an area of opportunity usually ignored. Especially fruitful for industrial firms, this approach requires close coordination across business lines but usually behind the scenes, as strategic capabilities from around the organization are drawn together to create new offerings. At Corning, Jim Steiner tapped into a variety of competencies throughout the firm, using his informal network of engineering relationships, and enlisted outside partners to create a new higher-value-added "window" for rear-projection technologies. John Wallace built a shared business model around idea–produce–distribute, pulling together capabilities previously scattered across all of the individual programs at NBC, to create a centralized system that improved quality, efficiency, and reach while replacing the individual fiefdoms that had preceded it. At Raytheon, Michael Booen combined three different technologies—missile detection, system control, and microwave—from different parts of the company and used them to design a new system, Vigilant Eagle. Each leader asked the question, "How can we, as a firm, leverage our capabilities across business lines to solve needs in the marketplace?"

Tapping into such opportunities called on the Catalysts' superior diplomatic skills, because it was more often informal networks of personal contacts rather than top-down mandates that drove such cooperation. Michael Booen even tapped into his contacts at the White House to get the Defense Department to release for commercial use the previously classified technology that Vigilant Eagle needed. True diplomacy in action!

Formula 6: **Networking**

FROM		TO
Stand-alone organizational capabilities	>>	A network of capabilities

---

Some leaders were even able to see beyond the bounds of their own organizations in order to create networks of capabilities that bridged organizations and drove organic growth for all parties. Chuck Culbertson at Schafer, whose story we told in chapter 3, saw the opportunity to leverage the company's nonthreatening status as a midsize player to move from competing for government contracts as a stand-alone vendor to creating Team Schafer, a robust network of smaller contractors. This network of contractors, all formerly rivals, was capable of delivering significantly better value to customers than any one of them could have done alone. Mark Spana at Hamilton Sundstrand, a global manufacturer of aerospace and industrial products, built "king teams" of multiple supplier partners, each of which was competing to be the lead supplier on an upcoming government contract. This ensured that HS got the business no matter which partner ultimately won the contract. These leaders asked, "How can we use external partnering to build scale and relationships that create more value?"

Formula 7: Starbucking		
FROM		**TO**
Product emphasis	**>>**	Experience emphasis

As we progress in our discussion from products to solutions, the service component grows, setting the stage for a near total shift from one to the other. This brings us to our final formula, which involves offering customers an *experience* rather than just a product. John Haugh at Mars/Masterfoods realized that the growth opportunity for the high-end Ethel M candy subsidiary was in moving from selling packaged chocolates to creating a chocolate-based leisure experience similar to what Starbucks did with coffee and Panera with bread. In such cases, the Catalysts asked the strategic question, "What is the experience I can create of real value to customers that leverages our product expertise?"

Making this transition often involves developing entirely new skill sets. As recounted in chapter 2, Haugh was brought in from the outside to complement Mars's extensive product-based capabilities with his service-based repertoire, developed through years of experience at customer-direct companies such as Club Med.

Regardless of which approach they take or formula they use, the Catalysts share the ability to *see current reality differently.* Each focuses management attention on deep knowledge of the customer and uses this knowledge to envision new ways to create value—whether by narrowing, broadening, or moving sideways; by creating solutions, new white-space products, or networks; or by shifting attention from products to experiences.

These formulas and the strategic questions that accompany them offer a useful starting point for a reframing exercise around any business. Later in this chapter, we'll ask you to try them out on yours.

HOW THE CATALYSTS REFRAMED

As we turn from the *what* of the reframed value propositions to the *how* of the reframing process, we return to Clay Presley. His success illustrates many of the key elements of the process through which other Catalysts discover and develop the value propositions that are their route to organic growth. Though each story is different, common themes emerge about the way in which each leader explores new possibilities, challenges a set of constraints, and manages uncertainty.

To See Differently, You Have to Be Looking

For starters, each of the Catalysts paid attention. Few managers in today's business environment have the luxury of spending much time looking at their business in new ways. They are too busy running it. A few lucky ones have opportunities show up and hit them over the head, but the odds on that are long. Despite all the hype about the need for organic growth, most managers are too busy answering e-mails, going to meetings, fighting fires—in general, solving today's problems—to look for anything new. Unfortunately, in order to *see* differently, you have to be *looking* in the first place.

Even the Catalysts, who saw themselves as builders rather than maintainers ("trappers," to use Raytheon's term, rather than "skinners"), needed a nudge. Poor financial performance was not necessarily the driver, as it was at Carolina Pad. But the impetus for ways to build dramatically better value propositions had to start *somewhere*. Sometimes it was an outside-in approach—customers came and asked, as at Corning and PDI—and sometimes it was inside out, as when Jim Steiner inventoried the capabilities at Corning and went looking for a fit. For some, like Conrad Hall at Trader Publications, the creator of an array of category-specific free classified publications, it was the dramatic recognition of the strategic vulnerabilities of his newspaper's traditional value proposition to classified advertisers. John Wallace of NBC needed to find funding to support new ventures in the digital space. For some, it was merely a corporate imperative, taken seriously, to drive the business to higher levels of organic growth. For others, like Michael Booen of Raytheon, it was an external shock—the 9/11 terrorist attacks on the World Trade Center and the Pentagon—that intensified the recognition that Raytheon had a solution that mattered for the risk posed to commercial air traffic by shoulder-held missile launchers. Some organizations, like Trader Publications, created processes that systematically asked managers strategic questions about their businesses and got them paying attention to customers and competitors at a much deeper level. Regardless of the source, these triggers provided just enough anxiety to allow leaders to create a sense of urgency that convinced others of the need to start looking for something new—or at least new to them.

Often, a set of aspirations directed the search. At Carolina Pad, the twin goals of "being the go-to company" in some area of demonstrated excellence and placing product in the top two retailers across all relevant categories focused their attention, describing the desired outcomes of any new idea. At Trader, it was the goal to create a publication in each classified product category: cars, boats, RVs, employment, and housing. For John Haugh, it was the ambition to transform high-end chocolates from a rare treat to a part of daily life. The Catalysts hardly ever waited to be handed such aspirations—they engineered them, often in conjunction with their teams, and used them relentlessly to focus attention on the future they wanted to build. This focusing of team attention and energy was a big part of their role as growth leaders, a topic that we'll turn to in chapter 6.

In the end, each of the Catalysts lined the team up at the starting block, made sure the finish line was well marked, and fired the pistol. And then the fun began. When the goal is to grow something from within, the track often looks more like badly marked cross-country terrain than a straight fifty-yard dash. And it starts in the deep, dark woods, where possibilities, constraints, and uncertainties intersect to reveal an array of potential futures.

Finding growth opportunities is part discovery and part invention, part uncovering what is already there (in the spirit of a business version of Sherlock Holmes, magnifying glass in hand) and part conjuring up something that is decidedly not yet there (like Merlin, magician to King Arthur). The Catalysts are relentless in both aspects of the pursuit. They are comfortable living at the nexus of often conflicting demands: the need to envision and make real a set of growth opportunities not yet in existence, and the need to recognize the constraints imposed by today's customers, technologies, and resources as well as the uncertainties that cannot be controlled or eliminated. These leaders are adept at working at the intersection of the three factors—finding new possibilities, challenging constraints, and managing uncertainties along the way. In fact, they use all three to increase their likelihood of success.

Playing with Possibilities

Few things are invented without someone asking, "What if anything were possible?" Of course, anything is *not* possible—any sane person knows this—but growth leaders recognize that the power lives in the question itself. Clay Presley, some might argue against all odds, *believed* that a set of new possibilities existed for Carolina Pad. Contrary to what a "reasonable" businessperson might have deduced, Clay believed that it was possible to move out of the dreary commodity business of paper by the pound to become the go-to company for something special, that a win-win solution would make "heroes" of their retail buyers, and that achieving widespread distribution in first- rather than second-tier retailers was not a pipe dream. What he needed was one concrete possibility that paved the way for these larger possibilities. He found that in the fashion notebook.

The aspirations he set out helped him define and bound a possibility space. Presley and his team at Carolina Pad specified a set of outcomes that would characterize a desirable future. In doing so, they brought to light the gap that existed between today's reality and the future, the gap that some concrete growth initiative would close. Arkadi Kuhlmann, of ING Direct, did much the same thing when he envisioned creating a company that treated retail financial services as a consumer rather than a banking business. In other words, he imagined how things would be different if banks treated their customers more like P&G did. Immediately, this exposed a gap between a future where products were simple to use, creatively branded and marketed, and supported by excellent consumer interface skills, and a current reality of complex products that were minimally marketed and where IT investment concentrated overwhelmingly in the backroom, not the front. He changed his business model in line with the new possibilities he saw, introducing products that were easy for consumers to understand and marketing and delivering them over the Internet in ways that were user-friendly. But where did the concrete possibility itself come from?

Again, inspiration came from looking both inside out and outside in. Usually, as at Carolina Pad and Mars, a leader's repertoire really mattered: Fashion was a concept that Clay Presley had seen work in a former job, John Haugh's experiences at Club Med taught him about delivering services to customers face to face instead of offering packaged products that they pick off a shelf, and Steve Oswald at Sullair cut his teeth in sales, so he knew how to listen hard when his distributors told him what they needed. For Arkadi Kuhlman at ING Direct, inspiration came from external scanning—spotting a competitor that was already trying out the idea. At Trader, the culture of idea sharing that Conrad Hall fostered encouraged a local manager in Detroit, far from headquarters, to notice a new publication targeting a different audience in employment classifieds and to bring it to Corporate's attention. For others, like Jeff Semenchuk at Pfizer, it came from "following customers home," spending time with them in their cars and offices and wherever else they went.

There are differences across our growth stories, of course, but constants as well. One constant was attention to the customer, or "Cynthia-centricity." Another was the Catalysts' ability to escape the prison of traditional mental models of "the way things work" in an industry and to challenge the powerful constraints that others in their industry accepted without question.

Necessity May Actually Be the Mother of Invention After All

All the Catalysts faced significant constraints as they embarked on their journeys. What led to their success, we found, was not the *absence* of constraints but the way these managers investigated, challenged, and ultimately *used* constraints as levers. Many businesspeople treat constraints as stop signs. They embark on a growth project but grind to a halt when they hit a roadblock. The Catalysts saw these constraints more as yellow lights: important signals that required some careful attention. Slow down and look both ways. They attended to constraints, not as unalterable realities that doomed an endeavor but as obstacles to be eliminated—in the way of transforming today into a better tomorrow—and sometimes as a powerful trigger to thinking differently.

Great designers and architects see constraints in the same way. Frank Gehry, the architect of masterpieces of design like the Guggenheim Bilbao Museum, sees constraints as important drivers of the creative process that set up the natural antagonism between possibility and re-ality. Constraints are not allowed to drive the design pro-cess, nor can they be ignored. Instead of forcing a choice between reality and possibility, constraints trigger creativ-ity by forcing designers to find *higher-level* solutions that break today's trade-offs and honor both the current reality and some different future. The Catalysts excelled at this challenge.

The constraints most faced were very similar to Clay Presley's: The strategic capabilities needed to execute the new initiative were missing, sunk costs limited flexibility, and organizational systems, processes, and culture pro-duced resistance at worst and inertia at best. Interestingly, these proved fairly easy to surmount—albeit in exception-ally inventive ways. The Catalysts were masters at finding partners, making tough choices, and skirting such organi-zational impediments as capital budgeting processes. But escaping the constraints imposed by financial resources or strategic capabilities was not the most powerful catapult to new growth. Instead, it was challenging the constraints *inside their own minds,* the often unarticulated assump-tions about business models. The power of mental models to either block or unlock the potential to recognize oppor-tunity was demonstrated time and time again during the course of our research.

Clay Presley grew his top-line revenues even though he was in a very mature industry. Executing his new value proposition required jettisoning the outmoded manufac-turing equipment and overcoming the lack of in-house design skills. To get around these constraints, he out-sourced manufacturing to more sophisticated off-shore producers and hired a young designer to head the creative team. That was the easy part. The hard part was opening the minds of his colleagues, who were accustomed to selling a commoditized product with a "paper by the pound" mentality.

For Conrad Hall at Trader Publications, the difficult part was, first, being willing to commit the "treason" (in the newspaper world) of giving the new publication away *for free* and, second, persuading Corporate to let him try it. Michael Booen had to convince the Department of Defense to declassify technology it had paid to develop (but wasn't using) and let him talk about the technology publicly and use it in a commercial product. John Wallace had to convince the *Today* show to give up its private production staff and share a centralized service in order to create the large-scale technology-intensive infrastructure that success in the new world of online media demanded. For each, the creativity, skill, and courage involved in changing the way important stakeholders *thought* proved to be the most significant driver of growth at their disposal. And it worked only because they saw differently first.

It is also interesting to look at the constraints that the Catalysts accepted—what they *didn't* try to change or challenge. One was customers. To discern what kinds of initiatives would be valuable for customers, they took as a given not what customers *said* but what their behavior revealed. In our research, we did not find much in the way of attempts to change customers. There has been talk of late, in influential books like *The Innovator's Dilemma,* about the risks of blindly following customers wherever they lead and building long-term business strategies around them. Yet the managers in our study did exactly this. Encouraging line managers to seek growth by looking far into the future can backfire, we fear. The Catalysts were not concerned with business strategy stretching far into the future.

They lived in the *present* and focused on finding opportunities to leverage today's existing capabilities and relationships to boost top-line growth *now*. Somebody in every organization, it is true, needs to be paying attention to the risks posed by disruptive technology, asking big questions about long-term strategic positioning, and placing big bets through new investments. But the Catalysts were otherwise engaged, meeting customers' needs where they found them—even if the customers couldn't always tell them where that was.

The final piece of the discovery and development puzzle we noticed was the way the Catalysts actively "de-risked" the new value proposition as they went along. Their approach, discussed in chapter 3, allowed them to enhance their control over outcomes and excite others about the possibilities they saw.

Instead of placing big bets, the Catalysts place small bets fast, which is something we'll address in more detail in the next chapter. The Catalysts play by different rules. As we've said, they have a passion for *both* worlds—corporate and entrepreneurial. They often choose to live like entrepreneurs. Rather than committing to new asset investment, they minimize capital spending. They leverage existing technologies, capabilities, and customers rather than searching for new ones. They leave it to someone else—someone in R&D, in strategic planning, or in business development—to ask those way-out questions, and let senior leaders decide how the firm will answer them. The Catalysts are about increasing revenues in real time, and they aren't distracted or slowed down by "big picture" issues because they see them as somebody else's problem.

At the same time, the Catalysts don't fight what others might see as the constraints imposed by the "mother ship," as some jokingly referred to their parent organization. Instead, they save their energy to fight in the marketplace. They often build their initiatives by flying under the company's radar—finding supportive bosses who provided cover to help them end-run rigid capital budgeting processes, onerous purchasing policies, and lengthy hiring procedures. They battle competitors, not Corporate. We didn't find a lot of pent-up frustration and tongue-wagging about Corporate among these managers. "You can't be anti-Corporate in a job like this," one remarked. "You'd never get anywhere."

The Catalysts are rabid practitioners of prototyping (another topic we'll spend more time on in the next chapter) and beta testing, and use them expertly, both to help key partners visualize and engage with the new value proposition and to test and improve. John Wallace chose NBC News to *start* the capability consolidation process. He knew that this part of the network was hungrier for digital distribution than other parts of NBC and would help him sell a solution to its counterparts—*if* he could prove that the process would work. So he did. Conrad Hall made one small acquisition—a classified publication—and made sure that he understood fully its formula for success. He could then replicate it quickly and with low risk, spinning the model out nationwide. Clay Presley hired a designer who looked a lot like the new target market to help sell the old paper guys on the new strategy.

All of these approaches allow the Catalysts to minimize many of the risks of their strategies, and pay off handsomely by allowing them to manage, rather than merely react to, the inevitable uncertainties involved in discovery and invention.

Putting It All Together

Successful = Reframing	Search +	Compelling + Possibility	Management > of Uncertainty	Power of Constraints
Results in:	Sense of urgency	Desire to pursue a particular choice	Control and confidence	Inhibited action
	Seeing current offering's short comings	Familiarity in leader's repertoire	Supportive value chain partners	Existing mental models
	New goals and growth aspirations	Intense observation of customers and competitors	Use of existing technologies	Missing strategic capabilities
Enhanced by:	External events	Vivid visualization of new possibility	Prototyping approach	Legacy sunk costs
	Discovering unseen pain points	Culture of idea sharing	Running small experiments	Organizational processes, systems, and culture

The Catalysts display both facility and comfort working at an often chaotic intersection of factors: They create a gap between current reality and a set of aspirations, they invent a concrete possibility to fill it by challenging accepted constraints, and they then "de-risk" it however they can, producing new growth initiatives with a high likelihood of success. The diagram above lays out this process and some of the key approaches that make it work.

In the same way that the seven "from-to" formulas offer a template for the *what* of reframing, this process offers a template for the *how*.

Taken together, the processes and approaches that we observed constitute a road map for the mysterious journey

	FROM	TO	KEY FACILITATING FACTOR	THE STRATEGIC QUESTIONS
DEEP DIVE	Commodity product to mass market	→ Differentiated product to focused segment	Deep customer knowledge Market segmentation	How can we get inside the head of individual customers to offer them something they personally value beyond the commodity product?
SWIM FOR THE SURFACE	Customized product for single customer	→ Standardized product for larger market	Prototypical customer New partnering relationships	How do we identify and reach a category of like-minded customers with similar needs?
SIDEWAYS	Current product	→ Adjacent product in the system	Exploit brand and relationships Infrastructure and capabilities	How do we apply our expertise to problems and products related to one that our customers already trust us to solve?
BUNDLING	Stand-alone individual product	→ Comprehensive multiproduct solutions	Work across business lines in real time	What is the outcome that customers are trying to achieve and how can we work together to help them achieve it?
FINDING WHITE SPACE	Stand-alone business unit capabilities	→ New white-space products	Leverage capabilities across firm	What can we do uniquely as a firm to leverage our capabilities across business lines to solve new needs in the marketplace?
NETWORKING	Stand-alone organizational capabilities	→ Network of capabilities	Build networks across firms	How can we use external partnering to build scale and relationships that create better value?
STARBUCKING	Product emphasis	→ Service emphasis	Experience-based skill sets	What is the experience that I can create of real value to customers that leverages our product expertise?

of invention and discovery that the Catalysts seemed to navigate intuitively.

CATALYZING YOUR BUSINESS

Now we'd like to turn to your business and use these insights from the Catalysts to ask you a set of strategic questions to help you get started on the path to growth leadership:

1. Using the chart below, try using the seven formulas and their accompanying strategic questions to reframe your current offering. Which ones seem to have the most potential?

2. What are the mental models in your industry and organization that might be blocking your ability to see new opportunities (e.g., the "old paper guy" mentality at Carolina Pad)?

3. For everyone in your value chain, working backwards from the end customer, describe how your partners define "value." Now assess how your offering is delivering to them something they really care about.

4. Lay out everything you know about the *lives* of your "Cynthias." How does your product help them with their problems? What would you have to do differently to make their lives even better?

5. Walk through each stage of the model on page 124 and assess your performance. Have you created a sense of urgency? What are your people paying attention to? Try outlining the new possibilities, constraints, and uncertainties.

5

SMALL IS BEAUTIFUL

Once they've discovered a new growth opportunity, the Catalysts move into action, breaking through growth gridlock by emphasizing learning by doing rather than detailed analysis and planning. They build their new business by making a sequence of small moves aimed at launching and learning simultaneously, and focus on generating data and insights quickly from direct market experience. These "learning launches" help them build a bubble that nurtures the new initiative and allows them to get out as easily as they get in. In this chapter, we'll look at why "Small is beautiful" works so well at producing organic growth.

Conrad Hall joined Landmark Communications, a privately held media firm with origins in the newspaper business, right after graduating from business school in 1970. He soon found himself responsible for business development. The job came with a daunting challenge: pursuing a traditional M&A strategy of finding potential acquisition candidates sufficiently undervalued or mismanaged enough that purchasing them would produce superior returns. Amazingly, many of his competitors in the media business (and elsewhere) are *still* chasing that strategy today as they search for growth. Even back then, it didn't make much sense to Hall. It was a strategy whose success depended upon either having proprietary information on potential acquisitions that other buyers didn't, or having superior capabilities for turning them around. Either way, market forces made it a small pool to play in—with limited odds of success. There had to be a better way.

That better way, Hall believed, was growing through a creative blend of *experimental* acquisitions and internal growth—making a series of small, low-risk media acquisitions in areas new to Landmark, learning what worked and what didn't, and then quickly ramping the successful businesses up to national scale before competitors took notice. One such experiment, focused on the classified advertising segment, was so successful that in 1991 Landmark spun off that part of the business, took a 50 percent share, and named it Trader Publications. Hall became its first CEO.

Driven by this growth philosophy, Hall crafted an organization at Trader whose strategies, processes, systems, and practices were geared toward learning and speed—a combination that proved unbeatable. Trader quickly became the national market leader in classified advertising across a steadily expanding set of categories, such as automobiles and boats. In the early 1990s, Hall and his team identified another "hole in the grid" (to borrow Hall's terminology), a place with unmet customer needs: employment classifieds. They created a prototype publication and began a series of conversations with personnel managers about it. What they heard was disappointing. "They thought it was a beautiful product," Hall explained. "It was creative and all the rest of it. But they just didn't think that they would use it."

The idea was shelved. Then, a year or two later, a Trader manager in Detroit noticed a new publication there that targeted the employment segment but focused on low-end jobs, in contrast to Trader's prototype, which had targeted high-end positions. Hall described the Detroit publication's appeal:

> It was given away free to readers. It was there on the streets, in boxes in front of fast food restaurants. We were intrigued by it, because the product had been designed to serve entry-level jobs, blue-collar jobs, service-worker transient jobs, not the high-end managerial positions. Well, lo and behold, at the lower end, the newspapers had become very, very expensive. You'd run an ad for a CPA, but running an ad for a janitor was pretty expensive. We realized that personnel managers were just desperate for a more efficient way to fill vacancies in blue-collar and entry-level jobs.

Sensing opportunity, Trader quickly acquired the Detroit publication and dispatched one of the company's most talented managers, Jack Ross, to Detroit. Ross's assignment was to decipher the publication's "recipe"—what made it work—and then to replicate it quickly. In a short time, he was ready to create an exact look-alike. Launched in Houston, the new publication became profitable in just over a month. Under Ross's direction, Trader was in the top fifty markets in the United States within two years, establishing itself as the only nationwide employment publication for entry-level jobs in the country— a spot the company still occupies.

Conrad Hall embodies the characteristics of many Catalysts: He is a shaper, a reframer, and an entrepreneur at heart. What stands out most is the way he epitomizes the spirit of learning by doing, an essential element in all the growth stories. Hall's approach to revenue growth in the employment classified business is typical. Having *seen* a potential opportunity, he moves into action immediately, using an approach that we've come to call a "learning launch," placing a series of small bets in quick succession, all aimed at learning from market feedback. When he's learned enough to feel confident that he understands the elements necessary for the new business model to succeed, he places the bigger bet, ramping volume up quickly. Hall's early moves—a mixture of "acquisitive" and "organic" growth—never risked breaking the bank:

Move 1: He prototyped the new idea, working with target customers, and then called the deal off when they didn't say yes.

Move 2: Alerted by his Detroit manager, he spent some time (but not too much) taking a hard look at what was going on there.

Move 3: He liked what he saw, so he bought the small outfit and deployed some of his top talent to "decipher the recipe," the essential elements of the business model.

Move 4: Ross believed he had figured out the components of a successful business model. Based on this, Trader tried out the new publication in Houston.

Move 5: The success they achieved in Houston gave Hall the data (and confidence) he needed. Trader moved quickly into a national rollout.

Like Hall, none of the other Catalysts view learning launches as one-off events; they see them as iterative processes during which they continuously improvise to improve the value proposition, through what Mark O'Neill at Kelvingrove Museum called "maze behavior." As he explained, "Rats don't *work out* how to get through the maze—they just try different avenues until one works."

In other words, these leaders are developing, validating, and executing their new business ideas simultaneously—an approach that appears especially effective at unclogging the growth gridlock we've been talking about. Learning launches allow managers to gain traction by building credibility and momentum through early "learning" moves that get traffic flowing. They focus on getting to volume as soon as possible, but with a *demonstrated* (rather than a predicted) success formula.

The type of learning launch that Conrad Hall conducts is just one variation among multiple options. Jeff Semenchuk's at Pfizer looked very different—beginning with talking Walgreens into allocating just a few shelves in a few stores to display hastily crafted prototypes of the company's portable medicine-cabinet products. For John Haugh at Ethel M chocolates, it started with opening four lounges in Chicago, each testing a different concept.

While all learning launches rely on leveraging existing corporate assets, John Zahurancik at global power company AES pulled off one of the most challenging types: *physically* starting up a new business within an existing one—working, as we've come to call it, within the "belly of the whale." Unlike Conrad Hall at Trader, Zahurancik didn't have the luxury of figuring out the recipe for success in AES's nascent BPL (broadband across power lines) business from the secluded outpost of a new acquisition. His bet depended on utilizing the company's existing physical assets—AES power lines in place—under the control of local AES operating units.

Zahurancik's aims were simple: to do what he called a level of "working due diligence" that would provide him and his team with enough data to feel confident in their understanding of how the fledgling business model would actually operate in practice. The concept of working due diligence goes to the core of the activities that take place early in a learning launch—the idea is to test critical assumptions as soon as possible. His original goal was to get to just one hundred users, enough scale to allow him to explore what he saw as the key underlying drivers of success in the new business. He laid these out carefully in advance:

> We wanted to be able to test a whole host of operating conditions. Some were technical specifications in the real world: Would it really perform as advertised? What would drive cost? How often did things fail or customers call? How many times did you have to go out to check on something? What was the frequency of unexplained problems in the system? In addition, we wanted to test a variety of products and services—obviously a basic fast data product, but also potentially voice, security, and video. We also wanted to really understand how much value a partner would bring.

The team chose Caracas, Venezuela, where AES operated a large utility, as its first launch site. They had the required cabling and a country-level management team excited about the idea. Zahurancik quickly discovered that starting up a new business within an existing operation was challenging:

> Our business there was a large utility. Processes that are suited to successfully running a large electric utility may not be particularly suited for a new technology-

related business. The people in the active operation have their problems, their priorities, and their budget and operational goals. And while one of them is to help foster the growth of business, at the end of the year they're going to be rated more heavily on their achievement of their operational performance than on helping incrementally move ahead a development opportunity.

Welcome to growth gridlock. It takes more than senior management support to clear the gridlock that builds up when the systems involved in running the existing business collide with those required to start a new one, as Zahurancik learned. He commented ruefully, "One of the things that I found most interesting was that we had *absolute* support from the senior leadership level at AES, and *absolute* support at the business leader level within Caracas. Yet you would find things just couldn't get done."

It took all of his considerable influence skills, a seasoned team at the local level, and a large supply of persistence to reach the team's first set of milestones. When AES divested itself of the utility in Venezuela, Zahurancik embarked on learning launch number 2, this time in Brazil. What he found was that the experience in Venezuela, though disappointing in its outcome, had built momentum for what would come next: "We took away some of the uncertainty by running a system first in Venezuela. And the project team found successes—they weren't fired or considered crazy. And so it's less risky for people to get involved in Brazil." The ambitions for Brazil were also a magnitude of order higher: "In Brazil we're doing this at a scale about ten times what we did in Venezuela—we're interested in getting to scale quickly." Informed scaling is their goal.

Zahurancik's approach, with its emphasis on testing

and small-scale experimentation, was common to all of our growth leaders, but we use these terms cautiously. The Catalysts objected strongly to using the language of "experimentation" or "testing" to describe what they do. In their view, they are launching new businesses and then learning as they go. Zahurancik explained the difference:

> We are starting a business. We are *not* doing a test. We're testing a lot of things. But the purpose is not a test. I think that's a critical distinction. The difference is you're not looking for a reason to stop. You're looking for ways to keep going. And if you find enough things to stop you, then you stop.

Initially, we didn't get why these leaders were so insistent that these were "launches" rather than "tests." The difference seemed like semantics to us—and they were clearly doing a lot of testing. Then we began to understand the difference in *attitude* that the words represented for them—a difference that lay at the very heart of their ability to carve out successfully a terrain between the world of the entrepreneur and that of the corporation, which we talked about in chapter 3. As entrepreneurs, they are *believers*—pragmatic believers always open to disconfirming information, but believers nonetheless. They are driven by a sense of optimism and urgency. As we discussed in chapter 4, they are able to see things that others miss. But they nurture their growth ideas in the world of the large corporation, driven inevitably by a fiduciary mindset occupied with skepticism and control.

William James, one of the founders of the field of psychology in the late nineteenth century, argued that the opposite of believing something to be true was not disbelieving it, but *doubting* it. The corporation's finely honed ability to *doubt* constitutes a significant obstacle to growth. In fact, the role of highly trained professional doubter is sacrosanct in many organizations. And it is the struggle between belief and doubt that can create the gridlock that destroys the urgency and momentum that new initiatives so desperately need. Our growth leaders see themselves as champions of belief and slayers of doubt. Learning launches are their weapon of choice, ideally suited to acknowledging—and then vanquishing—the deadly opponent doubt.

What was interesting to us was that rather than merely *deny* the fact that doubt existed or *debate* it endlessly in meetings, the Catalysts' process acknowledges the sources of doubt: They identify the key assumptions necessary for the business model to succeed and subject these to the most reliable of all tests—that of the marketplace. So, while they refuse to reduce their efforts to a mindset of "go" or "no go" (to accept this would be to embrace the attitude they fought), they focus their efforts on determining and demonstrating the conditions under which "go" makes sense.

As Zahurancik himself points out, this is a critical distinction and the foundation of the power of learning launches. In the internal struggle that causes growth gridlock, our growth leaders do not usually triumph by either marshaling the political force to override the doubters' vetoes or by coming up with superior arguments. Instead, they lay out their assumptions and subject them to rigorous testing. They invite the doubters into the process. Think back to the divergent personality preferences that we discussed in chapter 2, when we introduced the DiSC instrument, administered to all the growth leaders in our study. Catalysts scored higher on Dominance and lower on Conscientiousness than all of the comparison groups—executives, salespeople, and the general population. There are a lot of high Cs in organizations. This can easily lead to a dysfunctional dance between the high Cs and high Ds.

The high Ds' action bias makes them comfortable with ambiguity and ready to move with little data. The high Cs, with their tendency toward perfectionism and much higher need for demonstrated proof of an idea's validity, push back. This irritates the Ds, causing them to view the Cs as unduly timid obstructionists. The Cs, on the other hand, increasingly view the Ds as irresponsible. The situation deteriorates, and relations between them worsen, resulting in the worst possible outcome for the new initiative: It is both slowed down *and* deprived of the attention to detail that would strengthen it.

The detail-oriented Cs are generally superior at identifying the weak assumptions upon which the new idea is built—the ever optimistic "big picture" Ds desperately need their input. The learning launch goes to the heart of resolving that tension, inviting the Cs into the conversation to voice their concerns—but in the form of identifying assumptions to be tested rather than throwing up roadblocks to be dodged. It holds open the possibility at least of making allies, rather than enemies, of the professional doubters.

So, we humbly defer to the Catalysts' preference for the language of "launch" rather than "experiment" or "test"—and with it their optimism that they *will* build a successful business that improves as it develops, rather than merely answer a question, perform a test, or conduct an experiment. Craig Wynett of P&G best described the rationale for the addition of the prefix *learning* when he explained to us: "What I'm trying to do is to *learn* my way into it. I'm biting off reasonably sized chunks of uncertainty that only take a reasonable amount of resources to answer, and I just keep going and learning."

WHY LEARNING LAUNCHES WORK SO WELL

We have to admit that it took some time for us truly to understand the huge benefits of learning launches with their "Small is beautiful" philosophy. In retrospect, the lessons they taught us now seem very obvious. Learning launches are the pixie dust that helps new growth initiatives—and their leaders—succeed because they make it possible to:

- *Build a bubble where learning is easier*
- *Make "good enough" good enough*
- *Call the baby ugly*

Each of these turns out to play a significant role in enhancing the efficiency and velocity of organic growth.

Build a Bubble Where Learning Is Easier

Let's start with the obvious: Learning in action is hard, and most organizations don't do it very well. Although the quality management approaches now standard in most organizations teach that variation is the mother of waste, it's also the mother of invention. Therein lies the growth leader's dilemma. We found a strange paradox in how the Catalysts fearlessly exposed their initiatives to the outside world yet often shielded them carefully from the internal workings of their own corporation. Like parents protecting a child with a suppressed immune system, they formed a protective bubble around the new business. They built their own little world where the systems and processes designed to run and control the existing business could do minimal damage. Our leaders didn't expect Corporate to *help* much, but they did need it to get out of the way of their learning. Learning launches helped them operate under the radar, avoiding the corporate bureaucracy and the molasses-like quality it brings to decision making. They allowed them to make learning easier.

As we said earlier, the Catalysts didn't waste much time complaining about the downsides of life in their corporation: They accepted them as necessary for running the existing business. They did, however, often see Corporate-mandated practices as counterproductive in the growth space. But rather than railing against them, they just tried to avoid them. Learning launches made this possible. Pursuing a sequence of smaller moves granted the Catalysts a degree of freedom and decision-making autonomy that bigger ones would never have allowed.

What organizations *are* really good at is doing more of the stuff they are already doing. Though this often gets in the way of growth, learning launches capitalize on this reality by not asking the organization to learn anything new that it doesn't need to. They exhibit the kind of risk-minimizing behaviors we talked about in chapter 3— using partners instead of bringing up new manufacturing facilities and extending existing capabilities rather than developing new ones. Those approaches let the growth leaders get a running start with minimal investment, using what they already know how to do, and put off acquiring new capabilities until they need to. For a manager charged with growing a new business in close proximity to the mother ship, this is the logical place to begin. It doesn't mean that they avoid learning altogether—it means that they begin by using the known and the familiar as a foundation for it.

Making learning easy also involves keeping it local and simple, where feedback is immediate and unambiguous, and where corporate politics and layers of translation don't obscure the relationship between cause and effect. In *Made to Stick,* authors Chip and Dan Heath argue that avoiding unnecessary complexity is essential to creating ideas that make a difference.* Local efforts take what is inevitably a complex challenge—growing a new business inside an old one—and manage the complexity by allowing it in controlled doses.

Let's go back to John Zahurancik and his learning as he struggled to work in the belly of the whale. Senior-level AES managers at headquarters gave Zahurancik and his team the go-ahead to launch a BPL business in Caracas; they understood the concept and bought into the plan. But when it came time to turn the concept into something tangible in practice, reality on the ground intruded and slowed things down:

> People at the senior level said, "That sounds fine." Then we got down to the Caracas business level and all the rules of procurement, compliance, legal contract review started to kick in. Everyone can agree conceptually that this is what we're going to do, but as you get closer to the *doing* of things, a host of people internal to the organization need to reevaluate it again before you can actually *do* whatever it is you're talking about doing.

* Chip Heath and Don Heath, *Made to Stick: Why Some Ideas Survive and Others Die* (Random House, 2007).

"Think global, act local" is a powerful slogan. But in the world of organizations, it can easily play out as a demonstration of the law of unintended consequences, where many a good global idea at HQ turns into a local nightmare for somebody on the front line. It's not that anyone's intentions are bad; it's just that in the translation from the abstract to the particular, something goes terribly wrong, and it usually has to do with a vital piece of local knowledge that HQ lacks. Real learning under conditions of uncertainty happens best at the ultimate point of action, whether it is on the factory floor or in the customer's space. The sooner you get local, the better.

And the simpler the better. Kurt Swogger of Dow noted that "as an engineer you learn to model simple things and get it going and understand it, and only then start adding complexity. The simplest system is the best solution." The value of simplicity is a concept that is being rediscovered in complex organizations, where the haste to achieve big results can encourage the design of very complex initiatives, without anyone taking the time to model and understand the fundamentals driving the hoped-for outcomes. These fundamentals are viewed from on high and afar, masked beneath spreadsheet financials. The Catalysts were as impatient a group of managers as you've ever met, but they didn't cut corners when it came to designing early moves simple enough to help them accurately observe the key details of the system in action. Like the excellent risk managers they were, they didn't try to scale an idea before they understood and had reality-tested the factors necessary for its success.

The extraordinary simplicity of some of the Catalysts' early moves helped make learning easy. Wal-Mart sold only *one* style of Clay Presley's designer notebooks, John Haugh experimented with *four* stores, John Zahurancik looked for just *one hundred* broadband customers, and Jeff Semenchuk approached just *one* retailer with a very small request: a few shelves in a few stores.

But it was not only the protective bubble that made learning launches work. There was an attitude to go along with it.

Make "Good Enough" Good Enough

Learning launches do not aim for perfection. Expert architects use rough scale models of their buildings early on to help clients envision new possibilities rather than to represent actual future structures. This is how the Catalysts used learning launches—to borrow Michael Schrage's words from his book *Serious Play*, "as playgrounds, not dress rehearsals."* John Haugh opened four different kinds of stores—each oriented to a different chocolate experience—not because he couldn't make up his mind but because he wanted to learn as much as possible and explore multiple options quickly. As he describes his thinking:

> You've got one of two choices. You can do it the traditional, let's take two-plus years to do this, let's build a small concept store in a warehouse somewhere where we'll walk people through it, do BASES testing, and all the things that traditionally happen. Or you *just launch it*. And our motto has been, kind of "Eighty-ish percent right and go, and you fix it on the fly."

* Michael Schrage, *Serious Play: How the World's Best Companies Simulate to Innovate* (Harvard Business School Press, 1999).

The growth leaders offer a crucial lesson: *Perfectionism* is a greater obstacle to growth than lack of imagination. That is true not only for individual growth leaders but for the spirit of the effort as well. Zero defects may provide the right mindset for an established business, but seeking it will strangle a new one. The trade-off between "Get it out there" and "Get it right" is a false one. Growth leaders like Rich Combs argue that you never get it right *until* you get it out there.

Once you've been granted the right *not* to be perfect, you can show—or, better yet, *sell*—your less-than-perfect prototypes to partners and customers. And then the pace of learning really kicks into high gear. The Catalysts didn't believe in keeping secrets. They looked for partners right away, as we saw in chapter 3. "Fail early, succeed sooner" was one of their unspoken mantras. They were impatient to succeed but not so impatient that they failed to hear the marketplace speak. And the sooner it spoke, the sooner they could respond.

But how do you know *when* "good enough" is good enough? That question is not as easy to answer as it seems, and answering it takes us back to the role of data and our discussion of predicting versus shaping in chapter 3. Think of data as falling along a continuum of uncertainty, as in the following table:

"Seat of the Pants" ⟵——————⟶	"Analysis Paralysis"
Little data	All the data we can get
Significant uncertainty	Absolute certainty
Intuition-driven	"Proven" knowledge
Fast decision making	Slow decision making
High assumption/knowledge ratio	High knowledge/assumption ratio

On the left, we have the unknown, perhaps even the unknowable. Here, we operate on the basis of assumptions; decisions are based on gut feel, and uncertainty is accepted as irresolvable. The ratio of what is *assumed* to what is *known* is very high. At the extreme, this risks devolving into the kind of "seat of the pants" decision making that organizations create systems and processes to avoid. There is action aplenty—but not necessarily productive and informed decision making.

On the right, we strive for as little uncertainty as possible, so we make decisions on the basis of what we *know,* rather than *assume,* to be true. The problem at this end, as we have already discussed, is that pursuing new value propositions usually implies accepting a fairly high level of uncertainty. Seeking certainty in this realm risks a descent into the kind of "analysis paralysis" that gridlocks growth efforts.

All growth leaders must decide where along this continuum to place their data-gathering efforts. In organizations struggling with this tension, we often see managers either reject the search for validating data altogether or mandate the same level of validation for both growth *and* maintenance initiatives. The solution—getting the *right* data at the *right* time—is obvious in the abstract but not so easy to accomplish in practice.

The Catalysts show that learning launches work *not* when they succeed 100 percent of the time but when they produce learning around the truly critical *core assumptions* underlying the new business model. Our growth leaders identified *exactly* where learning really mattered and designed launches that zeroed in on producing knowledge there. The Catalysts let go of all the rest of the "nice to know" stuff.

Separating important from extraneous uncertainty is essential. Uncertainty, whether relevant or not, increases complexity and clouds thinking. Disregarding the uncertainty that doesn't really matter—drilling down to what makes a difference—is the key to clarity and speed in decision making. And it doesn't take membership in Mensa to identify the core assumptions that need to be examined; they generally fit into a pretty obvious set of categories. The first has to do with the value proposition to customers—the market side. The next has to do with the implementation piece: Can we execute? And the final one concerns competitors' reactions. In chapter 8, we'll explore each of these in detail in the design of your learning launch.

For now, let's just note that as growth leaders identify and learn more about the assumptions in each category, they *actively seek*—rather than ignore—the kind of disconfirming data that would cause them to alter their assumptions. As we discussed in chapter 4, customers can rarely *speak* of what they truly need but haven't yet seen. It is the power of observation that counts, and learning launches facilitate the observation of a new value proposition in action. One of our colleagues, David Newkirk, is fond of pointing out that although leaders may like to think of themselves as physicians who diagnose and treat patients' ills, they are really more like veterinarians, whose patients can't *tell* them what is wrong. A good veterinarian must put, say, a horse through a carefully designed set of paces to gain the insights he or she needs to diagnose and deal with the animal's ills. That is the role that the early moves in learning launches play in a new growth initiative.

When the paces work, the ability to refine and improve the value proposition is realized, as is the capacity to identify quickly when the underlying business model is irretrievably flawed. If small bets are to produce big wins, it is as essential to get *out* of new businesses quickly as it is to get into them.

Call the Baby Ugly

Learning has a lot to do with things not turning out the way we expect them to. The willingness to "call the baby ugly," as John Haugh of Mars/Masterfoods termed it, is essential. Much as we'd like to pretend otherwise, learning and disappointment tend to go hand in hand. In fact, we know that failure is generally a better teacher than success, if only we were better students. Jeff Semenchuk noted, "I've started four new businesses. Three succeeded, one failed. I learned way more from the one that failed."

The idea that organizations must grapple with uncertainty and take risks to succeed at innovation is widely *talked about* today. But we rarely see it practiced. With risk comes the inevitability of sometimes guessing wrong, of making mistakes. Organizations tend to ignore that. It's unusual to find managers who juggle with beanbags instead of flaming torches, who accept that inevitability of failure and design early efforts to help *identify* and *improve* their key assumptions. That is what learning launches are all about.

Learning launches maximize the ability to acknowledge and learn from the phenomenon we usually call "failure," because they are predicated on the notion that the only true failure is a failure to learn. In our research, the Catalysts' willingness to acknowledge that fundamental assumptions about the business model had been proven wrong and to act accordingly—to "call the baby ugly"—was fundamental to the success of the learning launch approach. Recall Conrad Hall's story and the first disappointing version of Trader's employment guide, which targeted the wrong category of jobs. Rather than dampen the enthusiasm for the next version (the one that proved to be a real needle-mover), that "failure" helped the team recognize the enormous potential of version two far sooner than Trader's competitors.

Yet even though we know that failing may be the most powerful route to learning, labeling anything a failure in a corporation tends to shut learning down. The managers we talk to often describe how hard it is to *start* something in a big firm, but they also admit (under questioning) that it can be almost as hard to *stop* a new initiative, once under way, until its performance is truly disastrous. Why?

We believe that the problem is as basic as the human instinct for self-preservation. In most organizations, career success and project success are inextricably linked. Though the *odds* of success may not be better than they are in the entrepreneurial realm, the *expectations* are much higher—unrealistically so. Venture capitalists are wary of an entrepreneur who has not yet experienced a failed venture; few businesses, however, are equally enamored of the positive benefits of learning the hard way. In how many organizations that espouse risk taking is it possible to count the body bags carried out after a failure? Far too many.

Because of this, only those courageous few hardwired by their own personalities and mindsets to innovate—like the "natural" Catalysts in our study—step away from the pack and try it. Building a culture of innovation in an organization, or just in your own business unit, begins with making the choice to become a growth leader a *sane*

choice rather than a possible career killer. Again, John Zahurancik offered words of wisdom: "Your challenge is always getting people to put both feet into the new
enterprise and run it like a start-up and not have one foot
back in the old business, managing their careers."

Denial is a powerful mechanism. How many of us see
clearly when our own survival is on the line, hopelessly
mingled with that of the project itself? The hard part is
developing the ability to look for ways to make the new
business work *without* ignoring or denying disconfirming
data. As we discussed in chapter 2, Catalysts with their
growth mindsets are good at reading signals from the
marketplace accurately while still believing in new possibilities. They are pragmatic idealists. They see the ideal
and engage all their energy in achieving it, but they do so
by acknowledging and dealing with today's reality—Jim
Collins's "brutal facts"*—not by wishing it away or ignoring it. They view some project failures as inevitable and
unavoidable and ensure that competent people taking intelligent risks are not punished when things don't pan
out. After all, the enemy of growth is often not *bad* decisions but *no* decisions at all. You miss every shot you don't
take. It has to be okay to take the shot and afterwards ask
forgiveness if absolutely necessary. But only if absolutely
necessary. A "wait for permission" culture just doesn't
stand a chance.

Learning launches emphasize speed; the idea is not to
dwell on anything but to learn and move on. Facing up to
the reality of disappointing results is every bit as important
as giving the go-ahead. Maybe more. If you can't acknowledge the truth, give up the dream, and move on when you

* Jim Collins, *Good to Great* (HarperCollins, 2001).

need to, placing lots of bets—however small—is a bad idea. And the process works best when growth leaders call their own baby ugly rather than waiting for Finance or upper management to do it for them. The baby belongs to the growth leaders, and until they are able to admit it's ugly, it's hard for anyone else to do so in an efficient and expeditious way. Eventually, of course, others will—but a lot of resources will have gone down the drain by then.

But how do you know whether today's ugly baby is likely to stay that way or is just going through a bad phase (recall your high school yearbook photo)? There exists an arsenal of techniques to help organizations make "go"/"no go" decisions, techniques such as return on investment and payback calculations. The Catalysts believe that these traditional metrics are innovation killers because they focus on the wrong things: price, volume, cost, and profit. They argue that, in the early stages of business building, leaders should focus first on understanding a single customer deeply, next on market size and costs, and finally on calculating pro formas. They see financial models as putting the cart before the horse. "If you do the financial model up front, it will be almost guaranteed that it will be wrong because you don't know enough about it yet," Semenchuk explained. "And the numbers that people do at the front end typically are all about highly assumption-driven, pure financial things."

The key metrics, for the Catalysts, usually have to do with the modeling of customer behavior, with a special emphasis on what customers will do differently when the new offering appears in the market.

Yet the Catalysts do believe in measuring progress and making plans. They set milestones and deliverables ferociously, and they use data to test whether their underlying assumptions continue to hold true. They willingly deliver the financial estimates that Corporate needs to put together budgets, even when they have to resort to the infamous "plug" to get the numbers to work. But they tend to view these efforts as a necessary evil, the unfortunate tithing to Rome. What they *don't* do is confuse calculating financials with the real work of identifying and tracking the behavioral metrics that they need in order to understand and develop the new business.

Let's summarize a few of the key attributes of learning launches:

- They start with an idea for a new value proposition to customers that has a clear shot at being superior to existing alternatives along some key dimension of price or performance.
- They feature two stories: a human-centered story about customers, and another one that makes the business case internally.
- They are simple.
- They involve a real customer as soon as possible.
- They emphasize rapid prototyping.
- They pay attention to competitive reaction as well as customers.
- They scan for partners to explore possibilities with.

CATALYZING YOUR BUSINESS

Now we'd like to take the insights about the value of learning launches and help you start thinking about how to apply these ideas in your own business. To get started,

	TRADITIONAL APPROACH	LEARNING-BY-DOING APPROACH
1. GETTING STARTED	Gather data and analyze. Collect extensive data and perform analyses to justify moving forward; form a committee to study the idea.	Just do it! Start acting on a promising idea and learn as you go in real time; talk to a customer or partner about the idea today.
2. PLACING YOUR BETS	Place big bets. Plan to roll out the offering nationally; build the plant; make learning visible and expensive.	Juggle with beanbags to start. Place small bets; conduct a local experiment; outsource; make learning low cost and easy.
3. PROTOTYPING	Expect "perfect" prototypes. Aim for prototypes that are fully realized and accurate models for subsequent offerings.	Consider prototypes as hypotheses. Don't expect to get it right the first time; expect the offering to "morph" as it develops.
4. MAKING MISTAKES	Punish and/or bury mistakes. Define anything less than perfection as failure; hide the mistakes.	Learn from the unexpected. Immerse yourself in mistakes when they occur; understand and leverage surprises.
5. SEEKING FEEDBACK	Keep it a secret. "Perfect" the offering before allowing users, partners, and others to see it; rely only on internal feedback mechanisms.	Get quick feedback from the market. Expose the offering to partners and users early in the process; create sounding boards to gather reactions.
6. PEOPLE	Focus on planning, not execution. Attend to the details of creating and planning the new offering, and leave the execution and rollout to whomever is either available or interested.	Test the offering, not the people. Use only seasoned managers to implement new initiatives; develop new managers in more stable environments.
7. INFORMATION SHARING	Disseminate strategy from the top down. View your executives as the thinkers and your employees as the executors; share information only on a need-to-know basis.	Create prepared minds. Tell vivid stories to customers, employees, and supply chain partners; invite all employees into the strategic conversation.
8. INFRASTRUCTURE	Assume that experimentation will happen all by itself. Expect creative managers to figure out how to work around corporate processes; give everyone veto power.	Make saying yes easier than saying no. Establish the infrastructure to support experimentation; encourage processes that support new initiatives rather than maintain the status quo.
9. FINANCIAL MEASUREMENT	Allow traditional measures to kill innovation. Insist on ROI and payback calculations early in the process.	Run the financials last. Focus first on understanding the market and then on measuring how big it might be; save the return calculations for later.
10. TERMINATION	Let the project die a slow death. Avoid acknowledging failures; let them limp along until they die quietly on their own.	Call the baby ugly. Acknowledge what isn't working quickly and terminate the effort.

take a look at the chart on the previous page to assess how much of your time you're spending in a traditional "business as usual" versus a "learning by doing" approach.

Now, take one or two of the new value proposition possibilities that you created after reading chapter 4 and ask yourself the following questions:

1. What can I do *tomorrow* to move the new idea into action and out of analysis? Describe your small move.

2. Who might I approach as a potential customer? Collaborator? Value chain partner?

3. What are the key known and unknown assumptions driving the new business model around:

   - **Customers:** How will you create superior value for them?

   - **Execution:** How will you create and deliver the promised value? What current capabilities can you leverage? Which capabilities are you missing? Where will you obtain these?

   - **Competitive reaction:** Who is likely to be affected? Are they capable of copying the concept quickly? How else might they interfere with your ability to succeed?

4. In each of the above categories, what new facts, if known, would cause you to alter your assumptions?

5. How will you recognize success? What are the specific behavioral metrics you want to pay attention to?

Later, in chapter 8, we'll unpack and elaborate on these answers when we design your full-scale learning launch.

6

LEAD WITH PRAGMATIC IDEALISM

———

The Catalysts don't go it alone. When it comes to managing their teams, they are a study in paradox. On the one hand, they are extraordinarily pragmatic—deeply aware of the realities of the situation they face and the skills their teams need to succeed, and uncompromising in their march toward success. On the other hand, they are idealistic—consummate dreamers who defy the odds to transform those dreams into reality by giving their teams support, encouragement, and inspiration. In this chapter, we'll look at how the Catalysts build high-performing teams that crack the growth code.

Pragmatic idealism is not for the faint of heart. There are no Caspar Milquetoasts among the Catalysts. The force of their personalities, combined with their extensive business experience, makes them uniquely suited to live on both sides of this paradoxical fence. From their dual vantage points, Catalysts are able to see what others miss, capitalize on opportunities, and engage their teams in turning their visions into reality.

ING Direct CEO Arkadi Kuhlmann exemplifies pragmatic idealism—perhaps to an extreme. He's a great example of what can happen when an irresistible personality takes on a seemingly immovable object like the conservative banking industry.

It was 1996. The place was Amsterdam, and the company was ING, which had risen in the global financial-services ranks through the merger of some of the largest banking and insurance companies in Europe. But ING's 40 percent market share in the Netherlands was being eroded by a new competitor with an aggressive savings product. The company needed to respond locally and to rethink its strategy for acquiring savings business in increasingly competitive markets worldwide.

.   ING seemed to be trapped—the company could either give up profits by repricing its products or lose more market share. But then came an unexpected move. The company began scouting global markets where it could turn the tables and take market share from dominant players in other countries. Setting up enough branches to compete with established banks would be too expensive, so ING began to explore the idea of electronic banking. It chose Canada, where branch banking was less entrenched than in the United States, as the site of its first e-banking experiment.

Enter Arkadi Kuhlmann, a former Marine who had made a career out of building and then turning over banks. He had taught international finance and investment banking at the American Graduate School of International Management in Phoenix, Arizona. He had been president and CEO of Deak International and president of the Canadian-based North American Trust bank, and he had held various executive positions at the Royal Bank of Canada.

In 1996, as Kuhlmann had just sold off his last bank and was ready to leave Canada for California, he heard that the ING "Dutch guys" were looking for someone to help them set up a new banking system in Canada. Kuhlmann agreed to an interview. When the ING executives told him they wanted someone to get a license, build a business plan, and give it a try, he asked them "whether or not they had staying power," and if they had the "stomach for it." They said yes to both, and Kuhlmann took on the challenge. Even so, when ING hired Kuhlmann to launch the project in Canada, its leaders had no idea that ING Direct would become the world's leading bank in electronic consumer savings accounts.

Kuhlmann committed himself to get the business up and running—and to break even—in two years. He knew the reality of the situation he faced: a culture built on the premise that banking is mysterious and complicated, and so of course banking customers need intermediaries. Transactions must take place at branch offices, where customers have to wait in line for someone to process their deposits and withdrawals and to provide other banking services. Kuhlmann saw the problems with this business model: high overhead for banks, which then impose minimum balances and fees on increasingly frustrated and impatient customers.

But Kuhlmann also imagined what was possible. He envisioned banking as a consumer products business, with a few simple online products that customers could procure at their convenience and without intermediaries or trips to bank offices. Even with slim margins, the reduced overhead would enable ING to offer a savings account with substantially higher interest rates than banks following the traditional model could contemplate. He believed that eliminating fees and making financial services more efficient would generate wealth. Kuhlmann saw ING Direct, as the new business was named, as a retail business centered on customer satisfaction. So, using HBO, eBay, and Amazon as his inspirations, he combined a retail mentality and online technology to create a low-cost, high-value e-savings product. His dream—"to make a difference in the industry"—drove everything Kuhlmann did. He was, as he put it, "very clear about the objective and relentless about getting there."

So how *did* he get there? What did he do to bring the right people on board, get them fired up, and focus them on results? First, aware of what he needed to reach his goals, he assessed prospective team members quickly against the competencies required to succeed. He hired people with a history of achievement who were "hungry" to achieve even more. He wanted people who were successful in their own right and had shown discipline in reaching their goals. That's pragmatism with a hard edge.

Yet Kuhlmann also knew that the business would require people who could see the world as filled with opportunity and the mission of this new business as something to aspire to, beyond the normal reaches of banking. Idealism mattered, and he had to inspire in the people he hired. So he chose people with a broad range of experiences who would bring a can-do spirit to the business. Kuhlmann was pragmatic enough to look for the requisite skills and idealistic enough to believe in people's ability to apply what they had learned from their experiences to a unique new business.

Once he got the right people on board, Kuhlmann put his hard-edged pragmatism to work by challenging them to perform beyond their own expectations. Unabashed about agitating people, Kuhlmann set clear performance expectations while remaining emotionally detached from the business itself. "It's not my company," he said. "I don't own this place. I'm in service here. I've got to earn the respect of the guys I work with every day."

Kuhlmann also demanded that everyone on his team be fully engaged and committed to the work. This point was nonnegotiable. "You are either in this thing or you are not, and I don't fault you for saying no. But if you say no, and you are here, you are wasting your life." Anyone who was holding back the team would be gone.

Here's a guy who was not out to win a congeniality contest. As he told us, "If I were a political leader, then I'd want to be liked by everybody. . . . But I don't see that as my role. People either love me and think I'm one of the greatest leaders they've ever worked with, or they absolutely hate me. There is not one person here in the gray zone in the middle." You can't get much more pragmatic than that.

Yet pushing people hard is only half of Kuhlmann's leadership approach. For all his toughness, he is also one of the most people-oriented leaders you will ever meet. His direct, honest approach, combined with his eagerness to focus on what's possible, creates an environment of trust and brings out people's energy and potential. This is idealism at work. "A leader's role is to make it human and to make it simple," Kuhlmann advises. "You can't make growth a constant. You can't put the company on the rack of growth. You might get that for a while, but you can't do it for five years. You've got to keep creating internal energy." And you do this by finding out what drives people, what motivates them to do their best.

One of the critical factors in Kuhlmann's effectiveness is his acceptance of people as individuals. He's openly demonstrative, giving people hugs and expressing genuine interest in them, but he is also able to separate *who* they are from *what* he expects them to do. "You may have a different religious preference than I have, you might have a different sexual preference, you might have no family, you might have a lot of family, and that's all interesting—it gives you color. But that's not why you and I are working here."

For Kuhlmann, leadership is about being pragmatic and idealistic at the same time. He's a tough taskmaster, ready to do whatever it takes to get where he's going. But, as important as the bottom-line numbers are, Kuhlmann also measures his success by how much he helps the people around him lead more meaningful lives.

Arkadi Kuhlmann succeeded where others had failed by taking advantage of an untapped opportunity in the marketplace. He built the bank in Canada and then moved to Wilmington, Delaware, in 2000 to expand ING Direct's business in the United States. Since then, ING Direct has become the largest Internet-based bank and the fourth-largest thrift institution in the United States, having achieved revenue growth at a rate four times the industry average. The result: 3.2 million customers, and deposits exceeding $50 billion. Kuhlmann's development of ING Direct in Canada and in the United States has become the model for ING's global success in the consumer savings business.

Like Arkadi Kuhlmann, the Catalysts display two contradictory qualities: *pragmatism* and *idealism*. In fact, their ability to thrive in the tension between opposing forces is one of the major characteristics that distinguishes Catalysts from other business leaders. We first discussed this ability to balance opposites, or tensions, in chapter 2, and have come to see this principle at work in how they hire and lead people.

So what is it about possessing paradoxical qualities that shapes the relationships and teams that growth leaders create? Let's take a minute to unpack the ideas. A paradox exists when two seemingly opposing ideas or qualities have equal merit. The notion dates back thousands of years to ancient Chinese philosophers who spoke about yin and yang—two opposing but complementary principles found in all elements in the universe. All the opposites we experience, they believed—health and sickness, wealth and poverty, power and submission—result from the temporary dominance of one side. In fact, the very existence of its opposite validates each side of a paradox. You can't have winning without losing or pleasure without pain. The two are interdependent, and their relative strength is always changing. Night turns into day. Happiness is overcome by sadness. Success is stalked by failure.

As we discussed in chapter 2, pragmatism and idealism are paradoxical, yet complementary, and growth leaders are comfortable living with the tension between the two.

We like to use a movie-making analogy to explain how pragmatic leadership works. As a film director, you start with a script and your primary job is to hire talent to make your movie a success. Of course, you don't just hire any talent, but the right talent, and you put people in their ideal roles. Some of this talent will be actors and writers, while others will be cinematographers and lighting designers. Feeling the pressure to please demanding audiences, you assemble your talent quickly, assimilate them into the project, and engage them in an intense period of collaboration, changing the script or even improvising as production continues. Then, at some point, you say it's a wrap. You release the movie, have a party, and move on. A few of your stars may stay on for the sequel, while others will go looking for their next role. If you're a really great director, some of your talent will want to work with you again and again.

What exactly are the qualities that you can develop or strengthen in order to build high-performing growth teams? Let's take a look at the three main components of growth leaders' team-building practices.

CATALYSTS HIRE AND FIRE EXPEDITIOUSLY

The Catalysts' top priority is to do what is best for their growth project and for the organization. Adamant about matching individual capabilities, knowledge, and skills to their particular growth requirements, they are matter-of-fact about making hard staffing decisions. They have few qualms about replacing people who aren't right for the project, pulling prospective team members away from other initiatives, or moving anyone who doesn't live up to expectations. Let's look at how this plays out.

First, there's hiring. Growth leaders act decisively to shape the team and the environment in ways that enhance their probability of success. They have a clear sense of the capabilities and qualities it will take for their team to succeed. Often, they look for some unusual quality that makes prospective team members especially wired for action. In Arkadi Kuhlmann's case, it was the individuals' drive and motivation to step up, own the challenge, and move at lightning speed.

For Michael Booen at Raytheon, it was a slightly irreverent quality that enabled team members to create the Vigilant Eagle program and take on the Department of Defense to do so. According to Booen, an ex-Air Force leader, his challenge was to "rally a small team of irreverent people like myself to go attack the naysayers and all the folks in the Department of Defense who said it couldn't be done." Another important factor for Booen was his insistence on people's willingness to tell the truth as they saw it. "You don't want people who will just parrot back what you think. You want diversity of thought, people to tell it like it is." Why? Because, he believes, "you've always got to fight group think, peer pressure, and all that good stuff."

Whether it's the willingness to take a stand, or the confidence to take on the world, growth leaders determine the qualities they need in people and move quickly to find them. How fast? Intuit's Peter Karpas assembled his team so quickly that it sent a "shock wave" throughout the company.

The Catalysts were willing to go to great lengths to assure that they assembled the right talent—even if the person they needed for the project was working somewhere else or was not at all interested in the job. At AES, John Zahurancik pulled every string he could find to get the team leader he wanted for his BPL project. The fact that Nicolas Maheroudis had other career plans, or that the head of global IT was planning to offer him another position within the year, were merely constraints to be overcome. Zahurancik called the global IT head and told him, "You've got to get me Nicolas. I need him now. If you need him in the next year, we'll talk about it then." Won over by Zahurancik's argument, the global IT head tracked down the sought-after employee, who was vacationing on a beach somewhere, and talked him into taking the job.

The bottom line: The Catalysts refuse to settle for anyone other than the kind of seasoned player they need. They are interested in testing ideas, not people. As Conrad Hall of Trader noted:

We're not going to take a risk on execution. We'll give
it to somebody who knows how to start something.
We are not testing that particular person—they have already proven their ability. All we're really testing is,
What's the market activity for this?

*Second, there's the rapid assessment of people's perfor-
mance.* Growth leaders form intense relationships with
team members and support them every step of the way—
even as they're continually monitoring and evaluating
performance. As Booen says, it's all about relationships
and risk. To assess people quickly and push what he calls
the "risk quotient," Booen meets with everyone on his
team at least once a month. "I reiterate every single time
that it's our job to take risks," he says. After setting expectations, Booen watches how people step into their roles,
always attuned to whether they are performing in ways
that meet the project's needs. And what if certain people
don't work out? They're gone, but with their reputations
intact. As Booen puts it, "We move them to different
places without the stigma of being fired."

Getting the best people often involves a willingness to
say, "Out with the old and in with the new." Clay Presley
of Carolina Pad moved out the "old paper guys," replacing most of the people in the organization in his effort to
transform the firm from a commodity notebook supplier
to the go-to firm for designer school accessories.

Rich Combs of PDI and Mark Spana of Hamilton
Sundstrand each replaced about 90 percent of the staff
they inherited upon their arrival, which set the stage for
their successes. Combs turned a single customer's need
into a new product line that now represents 15 to 20 percent of PDI's business. Spana transformed a business in
which projects were seen as overregulated and riddled

with technical and manufacturing problems into one that attracted "the best technical engineers in the industry," resulting in new contracts potentially worth $1 billion.

Most of the growth leaders have similar stories to tell. They quickly hired people they believed would contribute the most to their growth project and, just as quickly, recognized and removed those who were not compatible with their philosophy, lacked the requisite skills or attitude, or weren't team players.

Catalysts Demand Intense Engagement While Remaining Detached

Getting the right people in the right place is the first step. The second is demanding from all of them intense engagement and a can-do attitude. Deep involvement is what enables you to build a foundation of trust, mobilize people, maintain the integrity of your team, and ensure the quality of the work. At the same time, as we saw with Arkadi Kuhlmann, you need to avoid becoming emotionally attached to the business itself, or to a specific outcome or course of action, so that you can easily step in and modify your goal or how you'll achieve it.

The Catalysts talk about the importance of providing inspiration, motivation, and a sense of common purpose to solicit the commitment and engagement required to succeed. ING's Kuhlmann describes his role in articulating a higher purpose as a means of inspiration as "big, big, big," adding that he believes everyone "responds to higher ideals."

At Target, Doug Scovanner emphasizes the critical nature of having shared objectives, explaining that the environment at the retail giant involves "an enormous interdisciplinary sharing of ideas" and the "blending of complementary skills" to achieve specific purposes. And Tim Peters at Dell explains how he engages people by appealing to their competitive spirit, seeing who can be first to solve a problem. He adds that people who aren't motivated in this way typically move to other areas that are a better fit.

It's one thing to learn about the attitudes and actions of growth leaders from the growth leaders themselves. But how do others see them? To find out, we interviewed people on each of the Catalysts' teams. What did we learn about their leadership styles and their impact on their teams? Let's look at Peter Karpas at Intuit. One of Karpas's team members told us that he has a "huge focus on winning," along with an ability to "get the team to play to its strengths." Another team member described his boss: "Peter's ability to create a clear vision of growth and to consistently reinforce it through broad communication helped foster a motivating environment for employees hungry for growth and change." From these comments, we can see that Karpas attracts people who find it exciting to be with a "winner" and who are comfortable taking risks and pushing hard to the finish line.

NBC's John Wallace said that he kept people engaged and energized by continually bringing in fresh perspectives. He did so by rotating people through his team every eighteen months to two years. But he never transferred the whole team out at the same time. By keeping one or two experienced people and bringing in eight or nine new members, Wallace maintained the continuity of experience within the group while keeping everyone "highly motivated" and deeply engaged as he tackled the move toward digital programming. He also demonstrated his ability to remain detached from any one team of individuals, reinforcing the notion that what gets done is more important than who does it.

What was it like for Wallace's team members? One of them told us that Wallace "motivates those who work for him to do a good job," adding that he "has confidence in himself and in those who work for him," which "inspires those on his team to stretch" so they don't disappoint him. Wallace transferred his confidence to the people around him, which made them willing to push themselves beyond their own expectations.

But is there such a thing as too much engagement? Is it possible to become too attached to a project or its outcome? The simple answer is yes. Growth leaders must generate excitement about possibilities, but they must also avoid getting sucked into the emotional seas on which their projects must sail. They have to be engaged enough to connect with people and inspire them to perform, while remaining detached enough to make the tough decisions required to keep the team on its high-speed course. Like John Wallace at NBC, they have to put their hearts into their work without becoming too attached to the business or to particular people.

This distance gives them the perspective to determine the best way to motivate people, how to modulate the amount of anxiety within the team, and when to change course. It enables them to handle negative feedback without being hijacked by their emotions, and to make the business decisions critical to the success of their growth initiatives.

Chuck Culbertson, builder of the Team Schafer initiative that we talked about in chapter 3, is a good example of how growth leaders demand engagement from people while remaining detached themselves. He describes his approach as "giving people a springboard to be successful if they can," explaining that he provides a budget, a facility if they need it, and whatever coaching and training they require. "But they're pretty much on their own," he says. "They have total P&L responsibility, and responsibility for their client and their market."

One of Culbertson's senior program managers commented on how this Catalyst's hands-off style affected her. "He believed in me and let me do my job," she said. "When necessary, he assisted me in strategic decisions. He pushed me beyond what I thought I could do." While he made sure this manager had what she needed to stay engaged, Culbertson did not have to assume personal ownership and accountability for the outcome.

The Catalysts' ability to maintain an emotional distance from their work plays an important role in their success. Some, like Culbertson, lay the foundation for their detachment by being extraordinarily disciplined and clear about expectations and goals. For others, like Kuhlmann, their emotional distance is a function of their personalities and beliefs about the business. All of the Catalysts are intensely engaged, yet they avoid being emotionally hijacked by putting the right people, structures, and processes in place before starting a growth initiative.

CATALYSTS ARE TOUGH AND CARING

Nowhere is growth leaders' pragmatic idealism more evident than in their ability to be both tough and caring when it comes to managing people. They are demanding and unyielding about achieving results and are unwilling to let someone's lackluster performance jeopardize the project. But they are also good listeners and loyal to the people on their teams.

PDI's Rich Combs epitomizes this tough love, which, in his case, is rooted in his early work experiences. "I spent nine years at McDonnell Douglas," he explains. "Eight years at the plant working up to production supervisor of a new start-up area. I learned a lot about people and what it takes to motivate them. If you can motivate Teamsters, which I was able to, you can motivate anybody.

"If they had a problem, I listened to them. If they broke my rules, they got slapped—figuratively, that is. I was very fair, never personal. 'Here's the job,' I said. 'You get your part done, and I'll get my part done.' It's amazing how people responded to that.

"Most people are pretty decent, but you've got to be direct with them and hold your line. But it's not just saying 'Do it'; it's also thinking about the human dynamics of what's going on. That's how you grow. We more than tripled the production of our choke point, which was labor-limited in a union environment."

At PDI, Combs sets the bar high and expects a lot from his employees, especially the ability to take initiative. "I hate non-decisions," he says. "Do something. Don't sit still. . . . I'm tired of hearing *what* we need to do. I need to know *how*. What's the solution?"

Combs's search for solutions is powered by his drive to win. "It's simple," he admits. "We never say, 'Can't do.' We give customers an option, do something we can do, and never promise what we don't think we can deliver."

In the competitive and demanding electrical power distribution business, Combs has to push people to perform their best, sometimes asking them to do the seemingly impossible. But he understands that people work best when they feel understood and supported, so he goes as far as helping people with their problems. "The less they're worried about problems, the more they are focused on getting the job done," says Combs. So, as he did at McDonnell Douglas, Combs makes sure he's clear with employees about what the job is and then creates an environment in which everyone can shine.

To be the best in the business, he explains, "It comes down to treating customers and employees the way they want to be treated, the way you want to be treated. I make sure that whatever tools people need, they've got. I don't ask how much. It may be tens of thousands of dollars, but it's still insignificant compared with what we're trying to accomplish." And those accomplishments depend on the goodwill and top performance of all PDI employees.

Combs adds: "I value every person in here as much as the next. I can't do anything without them and they know that. I think we give them pretty good direction and we're aggressive at going after new ideas. But I know everybody on the shop floor. I know their spouses, I know their kids. To me that's very important.

The fact that Combs truly cares about his employees is well known throughout the company. "Rich Combs is the motivating force behind PDI," said PDI's controller. "He empowers his people to get the job done but always with the highest of integrity. He has the respect of everyone within the company, knows the names of all his employees, and is fair to everyone." As the VP of operations at PDI puts it, "Combs's genuine caring for the people fosters an environment where all employees care about the success of the company."

John Wallace at NBC is also tough and caring, as well

as fair. He says, "You want to be very, very fair, but you have to be tough at times as well. A lot of leaders become a little bit too warm and become the complaint box. I want people to know that I have an open-door policy, that you can come in, but we're here to solve problems. I'm not here to listen to the fact that so-and-so is not being nice to you." Delivering results is what matters.

Some managers are tough, rough, and ready to jump on people who fail to meet their high performance expectations. They are overly demanding and authoritative, always taking charge and rarely delegating responsibility or giving people the credit they deserve. Sometimes harsh, and often impatient, they can ride roughshod over everyone in their paths. Other leaders are too caring, bending over backwards to treat everyone well and often catering to the needs of individuals over the needs of the company or the project. They are sociable and charming; they value people and generally build great teams. Sometimes impulsive, and often indirect, they can end up running in circles—chasing consensus but accomplishing little.

The ability to balance toughness and caring plays out in the Catalysts' attitude about mistakes and failures, as we saw with Rich Combs. Given their demanding style and penchant for speed, you might expect Catalysts to punish swiftly any team member responsible for a mistake or failure. But given their respect for the people on their teams, you might also expect them to go a little easy on the responsible party. In reality, both are true to a degree. If the mistake is the result of poor performance or ineptitude, the ax is likely to fall quickly. If the failure is due to informed risk taking and occurs in the context of competent and well-intentioned action, however, the

Catalysts are more circumspect. As we discussed in chapter 5, they recognize that some failures are inevitable and unavoidable, and that competent people taking intelligent risks should not be punished when things don't work out.

These three sets of behaviors—hiring and firing expeditiously, demanding intense engagement while remaining detached, and being both tough and caring—enable the Catalysts to drive for results with a sense of urgency and shared purpose. They enable growth.

You might wonder why we haven't singled out the Catalysts' passion for results as a separate behavior. Certainly, it's an important part of what they do. Growth leaders live or die on the basis of their results and how fast they produce them. Indeed, a focus on outcomes seems like part of their DNA. It's an unconscious competence and a foundation for everything they do—both a cause and a consequence of their actions. It enables them to hire and fire expeditiously, demand intense engagement while remaining detached, and be both tough and caring— which, in turn, enable them to create results. And it all happens at maximum speed, something we will talk more about in chapter 7.

HOW TO LEAD WITH PRAGMATIC IDEALISM

What can you do to lead pragmatically and idealistically at the same time? The first step is to identify your starting point and your destination. What are your predominant leadership characteristics and to what do you aspire? Do you want to hire and fire more efficiently? Are you striving to get people more engaged or to keep yourself more detached? Would you like to be tougher or more caring?

To become a growth leader and embrace pragmatic idealism, you must, simultaneously, observe how you're behaving in the moment, test out new behaviors, and take note of your impact on the people around you. You have to both lead and listen to determine what does and doesn't work. Like the Catalysts we've profiled throughout the book, you must adopt a growth mindset and use anxiety as a positive source of energy for change.

The second step is to put together an A team. If you settle for B players, hoping you can inspire or develop them along the way, you will shackle your effort from the start. It takes the best people, fully committed to a shared vision and performing consistently at the top of their game, to execute a growth initiative inside a mature company.

Growth leadership is within your reach, if you understand that success begins with you and are willing to look within to find its source. It is important to note, however, that your outer success will be either helped or hindered by the organization for which you work and by your position and credibility within that organization. Having a growth leader's mindset can take you only so far if you're not in the right environment. Most of the leaders we interviewed were in sufficient positions of authority, or able to garner enough credibility or support, to launch a growth initiative. You may need to gain additional authority or move into a different position to put your growth leadership skills to the test.

After all is said and done, when it comes to building successful growth teams, our Catalysts are excellent teachers as well as lifelong learners. By their example and their leadership, they are a model for how to grow both themselves and the business. They understand that personal growth and business growth are intertwined and interdependent. So, to improve your business by 15 percent, everyone on your team must improve by 15 percent, starting with you.

We'd like you to start by assessing your current performance and opportunities for improvement across the tasks we've talked about here, using the chart below:

BUILDING GROWTH TEAMS WORKSHEET			
LEADERSHIP TASK	**WHAT YOU DO WELL**	**WHAT YOU CAN IMPROVE**	**WHAT YOU WILL DO DIFFERENTLY**
Assemble and reconfigure teams quickly, expediently, and from across the organization.			
Quickly assess people's capability and potential.			
Demand and receive intense engagement, ownership, collaboration, and accountability.			
Be tough but fair.			
Hold people accountable.			

Then, ask yourself the following questions to improve your ability to master the balance of idealism and pragmatism.

About Hiring and Firing Expeditiously

1. To what extent do I base my hiring and firing decisions on what's best for the project instead of on my own preferences or those of my boss or team?

2. How effective am I at identifying the right growth mindset and matching individual capabilities, knowledge, and skills to my initiative's growth requirements?

3. How effective am I in setting and communicating the highest standards to new team members and being absolutely clear about what I'm looking for?

4. When someone isn't working out, how quickly do I have the hard conversation with that individual and how comfortable am I having it?

5. How can I leverage my drive for speed and results to hire—and fire—more quickly?

About Demanding Intense Engagement While Remaining Detached

1. In what ways am I using anxiety as a positive force for creating intense engagement within my team, and how can I become more effective?

2. How effective am I in recognizing what it takes for team members to feel engaged, both intellectually and emotionally?

3. What does it take for me to remain detached enough from what I'm doing to make necessary decisions and changes quickly?

4. How often do I let the emotions of a team player interfere with my objective evaluation of his or her performance?

5. How can I balance my own engagement and detachment more effectively?

About Being Tough and Fair

1. Do I need to be tougher with people on my growth team, and if so, what will it take for me to do that?

2. How would people rate my fairness as a leader?

3. What would it take for me to be more adept in having difficult conversations with people about their performance?

4. Am I able to drive for results while being caring and compassionate?

5. What more can I do to support people without slowing down the business?

7

SPEED THRILLS

———

Put together everything we've talked about, and you'll find speed at the core of the Catalysts' approach to growth. Like the natural phenomenon they're named after, the Catalysts facilitate speed by reducing the barriers that slow things down. Speed is both a desired way of operating and the result of operating that way. It is also a natural consequence of assembling all the lessons we've discussed so far in this book. In this chapter, we'll examine why speed is the ultimate Trojan horse.

The Catalysts are *obsessed* with speed. Their passion for speed emerges as one of the most dramatic and universal findings in our research. In their world, speed is both an *aspiration* that lives in people's heads, requiring a sense of urgency and clarity, and a *capability* that produces action, requiring skills and alignment.

Assembling these ingredients in the recipe for speed is what Kurt Swogger's story is all about. He turns around Dow's polyethylene business by making sure that his team *wants* speed and is on the same page about what it means to get there. He works on putting in place the tools and skills needed to pull it off and makes sure that the organization isn't getting in its own way. In doing so, he demonstrates that what it takes to make speed happen— like almost everything else we've talked about in this book—turns out to be *different* when you are working in the world of uncertainty and growth instead of the world of stability and maintenance.

But before we turn to Swogger's story, let's look at how we achieve speed in environments of stability and predictability—say, in the world of fast food. How does a best-practices exemplar like McDonald's deliver on speed when customers step up to the counter? It creates a standardized and controlled process, aligned for and capable of speed. It drives urgency through a set of carefully defined targets, like ninety-second throughput. Presto! Crunchy fries and a warm burger delivered quickly and consistently. Time goals provide the push, and the process provides the rest. It's a system based on push and control. And it works.

Unless you want them to hold the ketchup. Then the system breaks down. Growth leaders live in a world where somebody always—and unpredictably—wants to hold the ketchup. It is more like an episode of *Iron Chef,* the quirky Japanese cooking show imported to America in which competing chefs are given just an hour to create a unique multicourse meal, improvising around a set of ingredients they are given to work with. Achieving speed in this world requires elements very different from those at work in fast food. It relies on repertoire, deep knowledge of ingredients and how they work together, and the ability to improvise. Preparing the mind to see opportunity, as well as the talent to act on that opportunity quickly, is the key.

In fast-food land, speed is programmed into the system: The system is designed for speed, and people then support that system. In *Iron Chef* land, speed is facilitated through people: People are designed for speed, and the system then supports those people. The former approach is about stability and control (sound familiar?) wired in beforehand; the latter is about awareness and responsiveness in the moment. Neither approach is inherently good or bad, but one is more suited for stability, the other for uncertainty.

Here we've laid out how urgency, clarity, skills, and alignment are achieved in these two different systems:

TWO ROUTES TO SPEED

	Fast Food	Iron Chef
Sense of urgency	Externally induced: time-based deliverables	Internally induced: wired into people
Clarity	Clarity of operations: based on rules	Clarity of intent: based on tools
Capability	Built into systems	Built into people
Alignment	Achieved by carefully aligning internal processes	Achieved by preparing and aligning the minds of employees, customers, bosses, partners

Now on to Kurt Swogger. We saved him for last not only because his is the story of a Catalyst discovering the power of an actual catalyst (how cool is that?), but also because he exemplifies the way the individual lessons that we've talked about in this book align to build a capability for speed in *Iron Chef* land.

When Swogger, a longtime Dow employee, agreed to become the global director of Dow Chemical's ailing Polyethylene division, his colleagues thought he was crazy. Even the consultant hired to value the business for a possible sale tried to talk him out of it, arguing that the polyethylene business, selling low-margin commodity products, was not salvageable. The way Swogger saw it, though, he had little to lose. He had both the appetite for new experiences and the confidence in his ability to shape the world that have become so familiar in our growth leader stories:

> Why did I do it? Because everybody said you couldn't do it, and it looked like a pretty interesting challenge. And what was my risk of failing? If you're in a big corporation and you take over something that's running well, what direction does it have to go? But take some impossible situation and there are always opportunities there. You've just got to look at it in the right way. We had assets that were sitting there already, so if you just make some stuff, and the asset is already sitting there, what's your risk? The secret is: If you want to have a big impact, take something that looks like a pile of manure and start growing roses out of it.

You can see the seeds of speed in this rationale: The combination of optimism, a desire to act, and little fear of failure creates a personal sense of urgency that is the underlying driver of speed. In order to achieve speed, you need to *want* it first. And nobody needs to give Swogger artificial deadlines to inculcate the desire to get moving— it's already part of who he is.

Over the next decade, Swogger went on to grow a lot of roses at Polyethylene, transforming it into the high-margin, high-growth Polyolefin and Elastomers (PO&E) powerhouse. Rather than a candidate for divestiture, PO&E is now the standard for innovation at Dow. And he achieved this by embedding speed, as both an aspiration *and* a capability, into the core of the organization.

But arriving at Polyethylene, Swogger didn't seem to be in a hurry. He followed his usual approach to taking on a business new to him: He got himself a steno pad and started talking with people—functional leaders, finance and marketing staff, as well as research scientists—looking for ideas and patterns. "Your people actually *have* the answers," he explained. "They just don't know it. And there's a piece here and a piece there that *you* have got to put together." Swogger knew that he didn't have the time or resources to build something from scratch—he had to get a running start with what he had in order to save the sinking ship that was Polyethylene.

The people in Polyethylene who unwittingly had the answers were its chemists. They had developed a new catalyst that would allow Dow—for the first time—to model and replicate with high reliability the process of creating customized polymers. Neither the chemists working on the catalyst nor other scientists in the group saw much potential in this development. Swogger, however, as a former customer and chemical engineer, immediately saw the potential for a dramatically improved value proposition. The lengthy trial-and-error approach the company had been using to customize polymers—with a 33 percent success rate—would now be replaced by a rapid and controlled process. Even better, Swogger saw that they could start with a customer's specified design and run the process *backwards,* asking the customer what properties he or she valued in a given application and then customizing the resin to provide exactly that. The new approach was named Six Days, to celebrate the dramatic breakthrough that delivered a customized solution in six days rather than six to twenty-four months. Like his fellow Catalysts, Swogger saw through his customers' eyes and knew that speed mattered to them:

What competitive advantage can you offer your customers to help them compete with their competitors? It's how *fast* can you turn around development time, which determines how fast they can respond to their marketplace. Customers are desperate to turn around their product mix. What you really want to do is use speed to make your customers the most successful so that they are afraid to be without you.

To deliver on speed as part of his value proposition, Swogger knew that he would have to make it a way of operating at the PO&E business. Speed became his rallying cry:

Speed gives you a driving force for your organization. We're not going to spend years on something. We're going to blow and go. And that makes it more fun and exciting.

He couldn't afford to have his people slowed down by rules that didn't make sense, so he instead created principles that would give people clarity around the desired ways of working but the flexibility to depart from them when they needed to. He developed work processes that he considered *tools* rather than *rules,* believing that "when you're operating in this environment, you don't want people chanting a mantra like Buddhist Monks." What mattered most to him was rapid results, not conformity to processes.

But speed didn't matter only to customers and employees. Swogger knew it was important to the bottom line as well:

I always knew fast was better because you just make more money—you just get stuff done quicker. You make more money if it's the right stuff. And that's the game. Because when you're doing new stuff, you're digging a hole before you start getting cash. The biggest variable—even beyond price—when you're doing a launch is how quickly you get cash coming in. The quicker you can get cash coming in and the quicker you can get the volume ramping up, the net present value goes crazy.

Making it all happen was not easy. Swogger thought carefully about which customers to approach. He believed that moving fast required finding customers *already* interested in creating and sharing new value, rather than trying to convince reluctant ones to try a new way of working together:

Any time you do a deal where you get one hundred percent of the gain and the other guy gets zero, it won't last. And you always get customers who want one hundred percent their way. That's fine; you just let sales work with them. You find somebody who says, "Let's do something together, and we'll split the value fifty-fifty or something that's fair for both parties." The game we're playing here is to recognize that the customers' need is fulfilled now, so you've got to come in and show them how they can make *more* money—or why would they do it?

It would take more than good intentions to achieve speed. Swogger knew that he needed to build the right skill set as well, and the staff he had inherited at Polyethylene was an immediate source of concern. He estimated that only 30 percent to 40 percent of the employees had the skills to play the new game he envisioned. So he quickly made the necessary cuts and then started assembling a cadre of employees with the skills he needed. Swogger believed that delivering on speed required placing people in roles that played to their strengths, matching what he called "how people think" to what the job required. One of his approaches was to look for a combination of people he called "starters" and "finishers":

> There are certain people who can spot new connections: starters. And other people can take existing connections and use them and make them better: finishers. A successful innovation is a new connection that makes money. The guys who make those new connections always want to go off and do something new again. But where do you make your most money? Doing the second one and the third one and the fourth one. The guys who do this—the finishers—have to have a pattern to follow, but they'll improve the connection, they'll use the connection. Those are the folks who make all your money. The starters create all your opportunity.

Swogger's "starters" race away from the gate to set a brisk pace; the "finishers" follow behind to stay the distance.

His other challenge was to keep the bureaucracy at Dow from slowing people down. His alliance with his boss played an important role in this by providing cover and protecting the bubble that allowed the new ideas to incubate without Corporate interference. Swogger also attributed much of his ability to move fast to understanding the way things worked at Dow, to knowing which paths to avoid and which to end-run:

> You have to learn the system, because if you know the system better than anybody else you get to manipulate it to your advantage. You might say that I thrived in spite of Corporate. But not really, because I knew it so well I didn't really have to follow all those rules.

Swogger was also proud of his ability to pull the plug, to get out of new ventures quickly when needed. When evidence accumulated that a given business was unlikely to earn the kind of return originally anticipated, he directed the resources elsewhere. Accomplishing this necessitated that people be able to "let go" of the projects they were working on. This became easier to do, he explained, because of the "invention machine" that PO&E had become:

> If you have only a few things and you kill something, then what are those people going to do? But if you have the attitude of limitless opportunity and you pull three people off a project, those people don't evaporate by leaving Dow because we need them on other projects. If you have that environment, then people let go of things a lot quicker.

In Swogger's world, the successful were rewarded, and project failures didn't hurt managers' careers. Only standing still—not trying—was seen as unacceptable: "If you don't try in our outfit, you're dead."

We spoke with Swogger just two weeks before his retirement from Dow, after thirty-five years at the company. We asked why a guy so wired for the fast lane had stayed so long in the same organization. Why hadn't he moved on to bigger and better things in the wake of his success there? It wasn't for lack of offers, he explained. He just never saw a reason to go. "Dow let me do whatever I wanted. They paid me well. It was fun. Why would I want to go off and be a CEO and deal with all that administrative flimflam when I was having a ball?"

THE NEED FOR SPEED

Where does the Catalysts' obsession with speed come from? Part of their passion is clearly *nature* at work; their personalities are characterized by a strong desire to get moving and little tolerance for indecision and anything that slows them down. Many of their self-descriptions include impatience as a defining quality. But there is more to it than that: The Catalysts also deliberately *nurture* speed, believing it to be a business imperative. Repeatedly they told us: "You've got to move fast." "I wanted to be there faster." "Speed is as important as knowledge." "There's a fuse burning on everything in life." "Speed is a mindset. It goes back to wanting to win."

Rarely did the growth leaders feel the need to spell out *why* they placed such a high value on speed. They thought it was obvious, and so did we. We assumed it was for the reasons that all managers are taught to value speed: because time to market matters. In fact, we came to understand that, for the Catalysts, speed is about much more than time to market for new products. None of the Catalysts believe that sustainable advantage resides in the particulars of their products anyway.

Michael Weisberg at financial services giant UBS put the nail in that coffin when he told us that time to market as a focus is "comical" in his business, given the rapidity and ease with which competitors copy one another's products. Then he went on to tell us that it is all about getting "from A to B as fast as possible in a streamlined way." We were confused, until we realized that it was his *learning* that moves from A to B, not his product.

Speed is more about compressing the learning cycle

and responding in real time than meeting artificially imposed deadlines. The Catalysts value speed as an *aspiration* and a *capability* as much as an *outcome*—it is as much a means to an end as an end itself. Creating a capability for speed—using it as a means to an end—requires lowering the barriers that slow growth down. This focus on barriers tees up the important role of speed as an *aspiration*: Speed happens because caring about it *disallows* many of the behaviors driving growth gridlock. You *can't* make speed a priority and still analyze endlessly. If speed matters, you *can't* endure corporate systems and processes designed for stability and control. Nor can you ask permission and wait for it to be granted. An obsession with speed delivers value not only (and maybe not even primarily) because shortening the time in which you do things is inherently valuable, but because caring about speed makes it impossible to follow many business-as-usual behaviors. It delivers an ultimatum to figure out a better way, to locate that alternative path.

Speed is a Trojan horse. In the daylight, it looks reassuringly familiar to Corporate as a source of competitive advantage. After all, who can argue against speed? Yet it actually unleashes a decidedly subversive force under cover of darkness. Like so many other accepted business concepts in this book—"customer-centricity" and "risk management" among them—what the Catalysts mean by, and do with, speed bears little resemblance to its use in the traditional business lexicon.

Each of the growth leader behaviors we have described in this book drives toward speed, either as an aspiration or as a capability. So speed becomes a naturally occurring outcome rather than a forced one. And because the individual pieces align with one another, all pulling in the same direction, they create an environment that makes it *easier* to move quickly. The Catalysts don't fight complacency—they just don't tolerate it. They don't send a mixed message—they communicate their expectations clearly. They don't muddle along with the wrong people—they put the skills in place that are capable of delivering on their promises. And they don't fight growth gridlock—they find an alternative route. They consistently find the path of least resistance. Consider PO&E's story:

- It is *easy* to achieve speed when people are wired to prefer action and to have broad repertoires that help them recognize opportunity.

- It is *easy* to form partnerships with customers aimed at co-creation if you start with the ones already willing to share.

- It is *easy* to deliver on speed if you are (1) building on existing assets, (2) matching the right person to the job, and (3) giving people flexible tools rather than rigid rules.

- It is *easy* to call your baby ugly when there are lots of other ones around to nurture.

Not a single element in the lessons we've discussed works at cross-purposes with the others. That's alignment in action. Let's look at how each contributes to speed.

The Catalysts' bias for action and a growth mindset virtually compels them to seek out new experiences and extract the learning from them, thus building a rich repertoire of skills and experiences. As a result, they see opportunities that others miss, execute them with a high probability of success, and further enhance their confidence in their own intuitions—which then leads them to identify other growth ideas more easily and more quickly. This virtuous cycle naturally accelerates.

In Kurt Swogger's story, it wasn't clear that he would become a growth star from the beginning. His first manager at Dow doubted that the new chemical engineer was aggressive enough to make it in the Dow culture. But Swogger's attitudes about opportunity (he sees opportunity lurking around every corner, even in the "manure" at Polyethylene when he took it over), his preference for action over analysis, and his wide-ranging experiences within Dow prepared him to quickly recognize the business potential of his unit's new catalyst when no else did.

Swogger has worked in every functional area, and his business-line experiences are equally diverse, ranging from plastic pipes and agricultural chemicals to Saran Wrap and Ziploc bags (brands that Dow later sold to S.C. Johnson & Son). In this last role, he'd been a customer of Polyethylene himself. This broad repertoire, like his personality, proves to be a key asset in achieving speed. The entrepreneurial approach also results in speed. After all, few entrepreneurs have the luxury of time. Leveraging existing capabilities is not only safer but *faster* than building new ones; creating your own future gets you out in front of those who are stuck reacting to their rivals. Affordable loss is a simpler—and therefore faster—calculation to make than ROI.

Swogger is the consummate corporate entrepreneur, seizing an opportunity that he doesn't have to *force,* starting with what is already at his disposal (the new catalyst) and finding a customer already willing to share the value and innovate as a partner. His moves are driven by a sense of urgency to convert ideas to cash as fast as possible, and he takes—or builds—the path of least resistance. Yet he is the consummate strategist when it comes to understanding—and manipulating—corporate politics. With the help of his like-minded boss, and the network of supporters he has carefully nurtured throughout Dow, he creates and maintains the protective "bubble" that allows his fledgling projects to escape growth gridlock and the paralysis it engenders. Once the projects are walking, he ramps them up quickly, delivering the NPV (net present value) that Corporate expects, and that confers legitimacy.

Similarly, a customer-centric approach—anticipating customers' desires instead of responding to their requests, giving them what they truly want instead of what others imagine they want—is also about urgency. The Catalysts waste no time trying to sell something created in the absence of market feedback. Instead, they invite the customer into the process and bake desire for the new offering into its design. While this kind of input might *appear* to slow things down in the early stages, it avoids the "throw it over the wall and hope" strategy that wastes time as well as resources down the road.

Deep customer knowledge is perhaps the most efficient route to speed, because a well-informed idea tests far faster than an uninformed one. Because Swogger knows how to look both outside in (from the marketplace) and inside out (from Dow's internal resources), he *quickly* recognizes an opportunity that those around him overlook: a new value proposition that connects customer desires and corporate capabilities in a powerfully differentiated way. Remember that he's been a customer of this business unit, so he is able to co-create with himself!

"Small bets fast" represents the ultimate in a process

that induces speed. Indeed, the learning launch is based on the premise that speed is crucial both as a capability and an outcome. Getting something into the hands of actual customers as quickly as possible—even a version of an offering that is not perfect, only "good enough"—generates the kind of real, concrete information that otherwise would trickle in much more slowly. Forming the protective bubble we have described—keeping the initiative's early moves small and under the radar, out of the path of corporate obstacles—bestows the freedom and flexibility to learn in real time and react quickly to new information. A learning launch is more than just a sequence of small bets; the important point is that they are small bets taken *fast*.

Finally, a pragmatic approach to leadership that assesses talent quickly, hires and fires when necessary, makes the objectives transparent to all, and puts the right people in the right jobs to start with, is perhaps the greatest labor-saving device of all. Swogger's leadership of his staff touches all the bases. It's all about the *match* for Swogger—putting the right people in the right roles. Some might call his housecleaning upon arrival at Polyethylene harsh, but it's what he had to do in order to deliver on his new value proposition. He believes that the business needs all kinds of folks to be successful, but they're not all suited universally to any job, no matter how smart they are. And getting the match right is essential to delivering with speed.

When all of these elements come together, speed isn't forced; it *flows*. This is why Kurt Swogger was having so much *fun*—why, despite all the challenges and frustrations involved in navigating no-man's-land, Catalysts barely seem to break a sweat. They're not frenetic; their version of speed has not a hint of careening out of control. It is intense, to be sure, but in a Zen-like way. They are immersed in the moment and focused on what they can accomplish in it, yet building a new future at the same time. And they aren't going it alone.

Relying on people learning and responding in real time, rather than on systems, to deliver speed doesn't let you off the hook for thinking ahead. Exactly the opposite: You need strategies and careful forethought as much as ever, but of a different kind. Aligning systems is the work of engineers; aligning people takes leadership. You can't calculate the alignment of people on paper. Instead, you need to seed the mindsets and skill sets that you will eventually rely on, preparing these carefully in advance so that they will be ready when opportunity arrives.

The Catalysts don't do this "just in time." They *prepare* the organization to move quickly to recognize and exploit opportunity by aligning minds around a clear strategic message, creating a natural sense of urgency around customer needs rather than relying on arbitrary time deadlines, and building the relationships they need to move forward. Like their fast-food counterparts, they create urgency, alignment, clarity, and capability—but in quite different ways.

THE CATALYSTS CREATE PREPARED MINDS

Turns out that it takes a village after all—a village of people with a sense of urgency who are open to opportunity, able to see possibility, and ready to act and improvise as necessary. Louis Pasteur famously asserted that "luck finds the prepared mind." Because the Catalysts' version of speed relies so heavily on people first and systems second, it requires prepared minds. The Catalysts work to engage the imagination and enthusiasm of staff at every level around the vision they see.

Storytelling plays a major role in creating urgency, alignment, and clarity of intent. The Catalysts love stories. Jeff Semenchuk argued that they are at the very core of the innovation process itself. Arkadi Kuhlmann sees them as indispensible:

> You've got to tell a story. As human beings we were educated on stories. Around the dinner table, it's all stories, right? Stories make things very human and not so abstract and intellectual. A leader's role is to make it human and to make it simple.

They tell inside stories about why people in the company should care about growth, like the "rice bowl" story that Steve Oswald at Sullair told to help his employees understand that their ability to put food on the table depended on the company's continued growth:

> You've got to think about the rice bowl when you're talking to employees. The idea is, "If we grow, guess what? We can invest in new products. That's good for our future. If we grow, everybody can get a raise next year. And that's good for our future, too. If we grow, all our futures will be more secure because we have a growing business, customers want our value, we're going to keep selling and keep moving forward." So it's about creating some connection between a PowerPoint presentation with a bunch of numbers on it and some employee sitting in the chair looking at it. It has to have a connection or else it's a waste of time. Unless you're senior management, the PowerPoint

means nothing. The story has got to be meaningful to *everybody*.

Creating urgency requires *caring* rather than indifference. A sense of meaning and purpose is key. If the work matters, *and* I matter to it, chances are that I'm ready to do whatever it takes.

But it isn't just to their own people that the Catalysts tell stories. They tell stories outside as well, like the one Emile Aarts at Royal Philips Electronics told about a new technology his company was pioneering called "ambient intelligence":

> One of my presentations was a story about Matilda, a character created by Roald Dahl. She's a small girl of eight and has the power of witchcraft and is able to move physical objects by pointing at them. She can control the TV set by just ordering it to go off or on. I made up a story in which Matilda loses her witchcraft and comes to Philips, where we help her develop her witchcraft again using the technology called ambient intelligence.

The Catalysts tell stories to anyone who will listen—to their bosses, their employees, their supply-chain partners, and their customers. In doing so, they make the new business ideas come alive. They make them vivid and visceral and create prepared minds in this way—using Matilda, or the rice bowl, or whatever works for them. They tell stories about the future and the unfolding possibilities that growth represents. And, in their stories, everybody has a role to play.

Colleagues of ours at Peer Insight, a leading innovation advisory firm, recently conducted a study that examined two sets of successful corporate innovation projects, one executed with speed and the other not.* The differentiating factors for the speedy ones—the importance of using real versus predicted data, getting customers to provide quick feedback, focusing on reducing barriers to early tryouts—echo what we've talked about already in this book. The factor in their research that stood out for us, however, was the extent to which the leaders of speedy successes told a "human-centered" story about the project. These were not stories about increases in earnings per share or attracting new target markets; they were personal stories about the role of the new business ideas in bettering people's lives.

Ultimately, the stories that the Catalysts tell serve two purposes. First, they create a *natural* sense of urgency among employees that drives speed. People want to help Matilda, or Cynthia (the single mom whose personalized M&M's arrived a day late for her son's birthday), or themselves. The Catalysts in our research rarely talk about using devices like artificial deadlines to *push* a sense of urgency onto their people. They don't have to. Their stories *pull* people toward the new future, like a tractor beam. And they can't wait to get there, because it seems important and human and not just an artificial target on a page.

The Catalysts' stories also facilitate speed by instilling clarity of vision, reducing the ambiguity and uncertainty their people face. Again, Sullair's Stephen Oswald offered

---

* Peer Insight's four-year research program focused on service innovation and aimed to identify best practices. Fifty-six firms, of which approximately 80 percent are Global 500 corporations, contributed recent service innovation projects to the research.

a compelling argument for achieving clarity through direct and clear communication:

> Everybody has a movie projector in their head. When there's a lot of ambiguity and you're not really sure what is going to happen, the movie goes on in people's heads and it plays all these different scenarios. And then what you've got is people watching movies in their head and not taking care of the customers and doing the things they should be doing. So I tried to make sure we had direct communication. When communication is clear and the situation is clear, then the movie projector doesn't go on as much.

THE CATALYSTS CULTIVATE CHAMPIONS WITH CREDIBILITY

Protecting the "bubble" that sustains the autonomy to drive rapid decision making is also crucial for achieving speed. The Catalysts' alignment with their bosses is key to this. Although many of the Catalysts describe corporate processes that are not helpful, none of them describe their own bosses that way. One of the clearest findings in the research is that virtually all of the growth leaders feel that they have bosses who run cover when they need them to. We know that you can achieve growth—and speed—in the absence of supportive corporate culture and processes; we have no evidence that you can do so without a supportive boss.

Most of the managers we work with (and probably you) desperately want Corporate to be different. We rarely heard the Catalysts asking for—or expecting—better Corporate parents. They mostly just want to be left alone. "I get a lot of rope," Michael Booen of Raytheon happily offered as evidence of why he felt that he enjoyed the best of both worlds. What the Catalysts want is the freedom to do what they think is necessary. And they accept the consequences of that. Rope, not sugar daddies, is all that the Catalysts need much of the time.

Most growth leaders, we believe, can do just fine as long as they get Corporate to a state of *benign neglect*. They don't need good parents, but bad ones really slow them down. Not that benign neglect is necessarily easy to get to—that is where the supportive boss comes in. Time and time again, the Catalysts told us why their bosses were essential to their ability to move fast and accomplish what they did. "When you have support from the top, you can build a business much more rapidly," Dawn McCall of Discovery Channel said, "because you don't spend half your time just *explaining*."

Sometimes, despite his or her best efforts, Corporate's radar detects a Catalyst's initiatives. Then, the lower the growth leader's own credibility in the organization, the more important it is to cultivate others with it in order to obtain the autonomy needed for speed. When Sanjiv Yajnik of Capital One was new to the firm, he found a way to compensate for his lack of credibility as he launched his growth initiative:

> There were key people in the company who had great credibility with the CEO, whereas I was fairly new. And so we brought those folks in and got them very close to the business to see that we really were going to make this work. They were monumental in helping us get the organization to a place where they started giving us more room.

Again, the Catalysts don't just *hope* that the support will be there when they need it—or dissipate their energy bemoaning their own lack of credibility. They invest in building relationships that will help them.

Ideas get to market for rapid testing only when established relationships with supply chain partners make that possible. Often, the Catalysts have to build these relationships themselves, independent of the larger corporate bureaucracy, which can be slow and inefficient.

Like the Boy Scouts, the Catalysts believe in being prepared.

Accelerating Your Business

Here are some strategic questions to help you put the concept of speed to work in your business:

1. Have you created prepared minds on your team? Your organization?

2. What stories do you tell? Do they include the human dimension as well as the business case?

3. Have you established a clear and coherent intent? Are your people aligned or are they working at cross-purposes?

4. Whose support do you need to facilitate the acceleration of your growth process? How high is your personal credibility with them? Have you invested in building a relationship with them?

5. Assess your own boss's interest in, and capacity to support, your growth initiatives. Does he or she get it? Is he or she willing and capable of providing the cover you need? If not, start looking around for someone who is.

6. Examine your processes for measurement and feedback. Are you measuring the right stuff? In a timely fashion?

7. Take a hard look at your planning process. Is it creating prepared minds and giving you the help you need to identify and execute on a portfolio of opportunities?

8

DESIGNING YOUR GROWTH INITIATIVE

Making the Catalysts' Approach Work for You

We're starting this final chapter differently than the ones that preceded it. There's no neat little summary at the top to tell you what is going to happen next. And there's no Catalyst story. That's because the story that's central to this chapter hasn't been written yet. Up to this point, we have been describing the attributes and behaviors that help growth leaders succeed. Our ultimate goal, however, is to help *you* find and unleash the growth leader in you. Therefore, you, not any of our Catalysts, will be the focus of this final chapter. It is your story that we are interested in here.

But before we delve into the nitty-gritty how-tos, let's recap how the Catalysts' approach to growth differs from business as usual:

The Catalysts' approach is about . . .	Business as usual is about . . .
Starting with what you've got	*Starting with a goal "out there"*
Actions in the real world	*Analysis in conference rooms*
Managing affordable loss	*Calculating ROI*

The Catalysts' approach is about . . .	Business as usual is about . . .
Exploring customers' needs	Selling customers your solution
Learning as you go	Rolling out a finished product
Being good enough	Achieving perfection
Testing assumptions	"Failing"
Calling the baby ugly	Dying a slow death through denial
Focusing on behavioral metrics	Fabricating financials

The end of each of the preceding chapters contained strategic questions designed to direct you toward the Catalysts' way of identifying and pursuing growth opportunities, and away from business as usual. In this chapter, we will put together all that we've learned in order to guide you through the stages of developing your own growth initiative. These stages constitute a path of sorts—a path that's different from that of either the entrepreneur or the corporate manager; a path that will lead you to discover the *best* of those two worlds and break through growth gridlock.

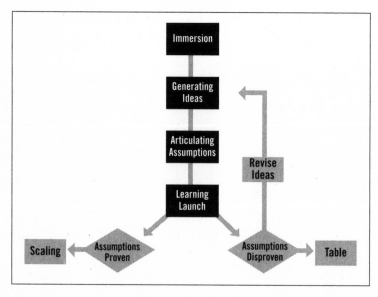

The Catalysts' Path

Let's unpack each stage:

STAGE 1: IMMERSION

Managers often succeed at growth opportunities when they start with what they've already got at their disposal: organizational capabilities and resources, their personal skill sets, the industry value chain, and current customers. But using the assets and capabilities that are right in front of you requires a deep understanding of them. Immersion is about closely observing all that's around you in order to build that understanding. It's about taking a hard look at your customers and what they truly need, examining the players in your value chain that could become partners, making an inventory of the internal resources that may be available to you, and mining your own personal experiences.

Begin by looking—and thinking—both "outside in" and inside out. What matters is finding where they *meet*, the place where customers and capabilities intersect. "Outside in" starts with customers. Growth, as we hope we've made clear, is not primarily about products; it is about producing value-creating outcomes for customers. Thinking "outside in" means putting customers and *their* definition of value, rather than products, front and center. Of course, products matter, but the idea here is to transform a product's theoretical value into an emotionally engaging value proposition for a particular customer or group of customers.

Looking inside out starts with you and your organization. It involves taking an inventory of your internal assets and capabilities, like Jim Steiner did at Corning and Peter Karpas demonstrated at Intuit. It *doesn't* mean repeating to yourself all the things you'd like to believe. Instead, looking inside out requires an honest, perhaps even brutal, assessment of what—if anything—really does set you apart from your competitors. This kind of soul searching is difficult, and few firms can pull it off without some help from an objective observer. We suggest that you enlist some of your more outspoken customers and partners to do this work with you, as Stephen Oswald did when he arrived to take the presidency of Sullair:

> I'd ask in meetings, "What do customers think about us?" My team would say, "Well, I think they like us." My response was, "I don't care what you *think*—I want to see data." So we organized regional summits around the country and we'd meet with six or seven distributors and sit in a room all day in a local airport hotel and just say, "OK. Bring it on. We want to hear everything—the good and the bad."

These conversations provided the insights into customers' needs that were the foundation for Oswald's reframing of Sullair's value proposition from a focus on selling individual air compressor products to offering guaranteed compressed-air availability to customers. Like him, what you'll learn will be more than worth the occasional discomfort you'll feel listening to candid assessments of your performance.

The value chain, the end-to-end system from the supply of raw materials to the delivery to end users, is where "outside in" and inside out meet the reality of the marketplace. Rarely is value created by a single firm acting alone, although we often think and behave as though it were. Instead, companies up and down a supply chain come together into a community of sorts, and collectively they produce outcomes valuable for the end customer. Unless your growth idea blazes a completely new access path to the end customer, you are going nowhere unless your supply chain partners decide to come along for the ride. Success depends on gaining their acceptance as much as the end customer's.

Consider the personal computing value chain. It starts off with the key roles played by component suppliers such as Intel (microprocessors) and Microsoft (software). These components are then assembled by "box" manufacturers such as Hewlett-Packard and Lenovo. The resulting products are distributed to end users through a variety of channels—retailers, online direct, sales forces— and then serviced by a sometimes different set of players, like Best Buy's Geek Squad. All these players working together deliver the outcome—the functionality of personal computing—that is the final value proposition to end customers.

But these partners who collaborate to create value are also potential competitors. They compete to divvy up the profits generated by the chain, and each is also vulnerable to growth moves on the others' part—moves that can benefit some players and hurt others. We need look no further than the devastation Intel wrought on its partners with the seemingly innocent Intel Inside campaign. Under the guise of co-branding, it effectively demolished barriers to entry and made it very difficult for even the well-known players in the box business—IBM, Compaq, and HP—to differentiate their products. After all, if what mattered was Intel inside, why pay more for Compaq's outside?

Eventually, Compaq was acquired and IBM exited the business—not because of competitive moves on the part of other box manufacturers, but because its own suppliers commoditized the box. For these reasons, analyzing the existing value chain often offers important clues about how to identify the most attractive positions, how to capture your fair share of the value the entire chain creates, and how to avoid the forces of commoditization. You need to consider all these elements when deciding where to place your growth bets.

We've illustrated a typical value chain and the important questions associated with it below:

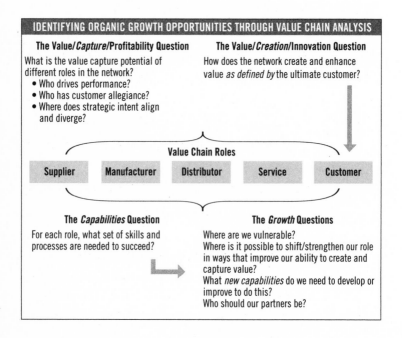

Using this illustration as a guide, draw the value chain for your business, laying out each cluster of activities, working backwards from the value proposition delivered to end customers. Add in all the key contributing companies, along with an honest assessment of their capabilities and bargaining power. For each box of activities, consider what the competitive environment looks like. Who are the key players? How many are there? What are the core strategic capabilities in each box? What does each contribute to creating value? Who has power in the chain? Why?

Having analyzed the chain as it exists today, consider what you've learned about the relationship between power and position in the chain. This sets the stage for thinking about growth possibilities and their likely attractiveness. Where do you see opportunities for improving your power and profitability by altering your position in the existing chain? Where are you vulnerable to others who might change their position in ways that put you at a disadvantage?

Finally, the challenge is to put it all together—matching the customer needs you've observed, the value chain realities you've assessed, and your firm's competency set. You may find that you already have the capabilities, assets, and relationships to develop a number of attractive new value propositions, but there are often missing pieces—new skills and partnerships that need developing, old ways of thinking that need abandoning, and other challenges that needed surmounting.

Stepping back to observe, honestly and nonjudgmentally, each of these three core elements—customers, capabilities, and value chain dynamics—as they exist *today* is the first step in generating better possibilities for tomorrow.

STAGE 2: GENERATING IDEAS

Having identified some areas of possibility, the challenge now is to select a promising new business idea and get to work. Chapter 4 focused on how to begin thinking about opportunities by using seven formulas for reframing. Immersing yourself in today's realities in Stage 1 should provide some additional perspectives to help you select the idea that you believe—given the data you've got—is likely to be the most promising. In this stage, we'll work to translate your idea into a detailed business model that can be tested in a learning launch.

In a sense, we will be building a *prototype* of your idea. This is a challenging task. Although we are quite familiar with prototyping new products, prototyping new *ideas* is trickier.

Fortunately, we can call on an approach that has been used for centuries—actually, it has been used for almost a thousand years. It is called the scientific method. Credit for devising the modern scientific method is generally given to Descartes, Bacon, and Newton (the famous apple guy *before* Steve Jobs), though Sherlock Holmes is probably its most famous practitioner. As we think you'll see, the scientific method is more valuable for a growth leader than more commonly used business-focused frameworks, whether old chestnuts like SWOT or hot new ones like Blue Ocean strategy.

The Scientific Method

In the United States, we are introduced to the scientific method in the fourth grade. Unfortunately, most of us forget it by the fifth. The only mainstream businesspeople who use the scientific method regularly are strategy consultants, because it is the backbone of their problem-solving approach.

The scientific method calls on both creative and analytic thinking. That is what makes it such a useful tool for considering new opportunities, an activity that requires us to be both imaginative in the search for possibilities *and* rigorous in figuring out which to pursue. Unlike brainstorming, it doesn't ask us to leave our analytical minds at the door. It invites *both* the left and the right brain into the process, and it is custom-made to deal with situations involving a lot of unknowns.

The scientific method accomplishes all of the above by relying on sequential hypothesis generating and testing. It starts with hypothesis *generating*, asking a "what if" question. This allows you to identify a new possibility, which is your hypothesis: an educated guess about something you *think* is likely to be a good idea. Think about Craig Wynett at P&G and the growth initiative that became the Swiffer. This innovative product was based on the question, "What if the mop—as well as the detergent—mattered in cleaning your floor?" That's the creative part. Then, to *test* the hypothesis, you specify what scientists call the "boundary conditions." You ask, "Under what conditions would that hypothesis in fact be a good idea?" Or, worded differently, "What would *need* to be true in order for my idea to be a good one?" You surface the assumptions underlying your hypothesis, and then you find the appropriate data to test them. That is the analytic part. In the Swiffer case, that would include testing assumptions like the one that P&G could actually *make* a better mop that would result in a cleaner floor and another one that customers out there would want to buy it. That's all there is to the process.

The benefits of the scientific method are extraordinary. The process is "intelligently opportunistic" because it lets you rigorously examine your current best guess, but not in a way that forces you to accept or reject it. Instead, the process allows new and previously unanticipated *improvements* to your idea to emerge. When Trader's original idea for a classified employment publication didn't attract the audience the company had targeted, Conrad Hall didn't kill the idea. He let it lie and then resurrected it when a refinement to the original hypothesis—targeting a different segment—came across Trader's radar screen. The process doesn't expect that you'll get it right the first time, and it helps you out when you don't. For instance, if it turns out that your assumptions are *not* true—that is, your hypothesis is *disproved*—then you go back and make your original hypothesis better. And then you test that new and improved hypothesis. It is meant to be an iterative process, so with each pass you learn something that helps you develop a better hypothesis for the next pass. You stop when you believe that your hypothesis is good enough.

The hypothesis-driven approach is based on *learning,* rather than *knowing.* As a result, it is particularly useful when we don't know as much as we'd like to—when, in fact, being a *knower* tends to get us into big trouble and being a *learner* is far safer. And although we think of scientists like Einstein as being consummate knowers, *all* major discoveries in science involve getting at least some of what scientists already know out of the way so that they can see differently and learn new things.

Does all of this sound familiar? Of course it does. A new business idea is, in fact, just a hypothesis. And a learning launch is just a process for testing and improving that hypothesis. We've already talked about the importance of *seeing differently* in chapter 4; that is what allowed the Catalysts to generate a new value proposition, to escape from their industries' mental models and see new possibilities. They see what others, who insist on "knowing," cannot see. Holding knowing at bay is just as essential for growth leaders as it is for scientists.

Let's detour a minute back to strategy consultants. One of the reasons why the experienced ones are so valuable is that they develop great repertoires, filled not just with business skills but with skills related to hypothesis generating and testing. They spend their careers answering questions that their clients think are important but feel that they don't have the skills to answer on their own. Say you're a manager lucky enough to have a revolutionary new product that you're ready to introduce. Thinking through the rollout is complicated, because you also have the leading market share in the existing product. Roll out the new one too fast and you cannibalize your own product and maybe make your existing manufacturing capacity obsolete. But move too slowly and you give up the chance to gain share points fast—you give your competitors time to catch you. Chances are, you will face this kind of situation only once or twice in your whole career. But a strategy consultant might deal with this situation several times a year and in a lot of different industries. The problem is *familiar* to him or her, so he or she has a repertoire for how to deal with it that you *can't* have— your past experience hasn't prepared you for this. That doesn't mean that you won't get the rollout right eventually, but it does mean that, on the initial attempt, the consultant is likely to be able to develop a *better* hypothesis than you are (he or she knows the "shape" of the problem) and to know more about what to test and how to do it.

Consultants go through this process under conditions that old Sir Isaac Newton and Sherlock Holmes didn't have to face: Strategy consultants have to test hypotheses about the *future,* not the past or the present. Growth leaders face the same challenge. Think about it. Gravity existed long before the falling apple helped Newton describe it. The crime has been committed by the time Holmes is called in to solve it. But unlike scientists or detectives, who aim primarily to understand or explain something that has already taken place, consultants are hired to change the present. Scientists and detectives *uncover* the truth, but growth leaders have to *invent* the future.

That's the rub. We talked earlier about the bind growth leaders get into when the organization's doubters demand proof that the growth idea is a winner. Providing such proof is impossible. Hypotheses about the future can never really be *proven* to be true. As a strategist—or a growth leader—the best you can do is marshal evidence from today that supports the argument that your view, your "story" about the future, is likely to be worth pursuing. Your argument has to be testable with today's data. That means that you have to tie the hypothesis about the future to some phenomena at work today. Then you have to ask your audience to leap with you to tomorrow. Their willingness to take that leap will depend on how compelling you can make your story about tomorrow, based on what you know about today. But only the passage of time can *prove* you right or wrong.

Your job as a growth leader is to *create* the future that proves your hypothesis.

But there's a further complication: It is almost always safer to treat something as a hypothesis rather than as a truth, but we can't afford to do that. Testing *everything* we think is true is not practical. Useful data are often expensive (despite all the garbage floating around on the Internet and the reports that accounting systems churn out), and testing everything really slows down decision making. The ability to determine *what* to test and *how* to test it versus what to accept as given is a matter of judgment. And it's a crucial skill for a strategy consultant or a growth leader, because inventing the future—as we've said repeatedly—involves dealing with significantly more uncertainty than running an existing business.

Hopefully we've now convinced you that it is worth

giving the scientific method a shot to help you deal with the unavoidable uncertainty of growth. What does it take to translate a good *business idea* into a good *hypothesis*? Practice. A good hypothesis has a clear set of characteristics:

1. **A good hypothesis is *testable*.** This is the big kahuna. A hypothesis that can't be tested is useless; in other words, if you can't bring data to bear on it, keep working. Ninety percent of the supposed "hypotheses" generated by the managers we work with fail this first test. They are abstract ideas, not hypotheses.

   The new business idea must be testable for a specific set of characteristics that determine the attractiveness of any business. These are:

   Value: Someone will buy it—at a price that works.

   Execution: You can create and deliver it—at a cost that works.

   Scalability: If you accomplish both value and execution, eventually (the sooner the better) you can build some scale.

   Defensibility: After you satisfy the points above, competitors can't easily erode the gains you've made.

   Eventually, you will want to test for all four characteristics, but not necessarily all at once. The value test tends to dominate early moves, because it is the one that turbocharging initiatives fail most often. Execution is usually less of an issue; scalability and defensibility come later.

The most common pitfall we see is calling an idea for a new *product* a hypothesis. A new product idea *never* constitutes a testable hypothesis. You can't test the value, scalability, or defensibility of a new product. It will only allow testing of the execution requirement—and that is the one least likely to produce a failure. A value proposition gives you more to work with, but even that will take you only so far. The only truly testable hypothesis for our purposes comes in the form of the description of a *business model*—one that specifies the value proposition and the customer it targets, the strategic capabilities needed to execute it, and the functional strategy it will take to create those capabilities.

We've already mentioned Peter Karpas's work at Intuit, which led to the creation of the Quicken Medical Expense Manager product. It's a great example of why the product alone is not the focus early on. He describes how he and his team thought about the new opportunity:

> It started with a big unmet customer need that we thought we could solve well and where we could get competitive advantage over time. The big unmet need [in health care] is "What do I do with this piece of paper when I get it in the mail?" Think about how precise that is. People are not saying, "Wow! I need Quicken Medical Expense Manager!" They are saying, "I need to track my expenses. I need to know what to pay."

Kapas's team couldn't use the Medical Expense Manager *product* as a hypothesis to test the potential viability of the business idea. But they could—and needed to—test whether the underlying customer need (stated as precisely as possible) was in fact there, whether the product as designed met that need, whether it leveraged Intuit's existing capabilities, and whether, if they succeeded at all of the above, they were likely to gain an attractive and defensible source of advantage.

2. **A good hypothesis is *specific*.** In order to be testable, a business idea must be specific. It also must be possible to confirm or disconfirm the assumptions underlying the idea. The two go hand in hand. Without sufficient detail on key elements—like the specific group of customers you will target—the results of any tests will be as vague as your hypothesis. And descriptors like "current" customers don't work. You will be tempted to state the market as broadly as possible. Don't. You will get your chance to demonstrate that there is a broad market in later moves, when you redesign your business model for scaling. In your early moves, the goal is to design as simple and specific a test as possible.

   The value proposition must be as concrete as the customer set. You want to establish that this value proposition is superior to what the customer can already buy, that it solves a high-priority need better, faster, or less expensively than currently available solutions. You'll also want to establish that customers have the money to buy the product at a price attractive to you and that they will actually hand that money over to you when the opportunity presents itself.

   The best proof of this, of course, comes from having the customer hand over money right now—or something else of value, such as time or investment dollars. That is the gold standard. It is also one of the benefits of co-creation. This approach ratchets up customers' level of commitment, giving them skin in the game, as we talked about in chapter 3. It is important to note that *asking* customers or a focus group if they will buy is a weak and vastly inferior form of this test. It doesn't separate the real customer from his or her evil twin: the "potential" customer.

3. **A good hypothesis is *not self-evident*.** This one we are throwing in just to save you time. Technically, you could create and test a completely obvious—but specific—business model. But why would you want to? Think about it: What kind of hypotheses did Sherlock Holmes like best? Never the obvious ones. You don't build your career as a famous detective—or as a growth leader—by taking on the obvious. It is fine for the hypothesis to look self-evident *in retrospect.* The best ones generally do. But not up front. If it is obvious *and* valuable *and* doable, someone else will have done it already.

   Of course, your definition of "obvious" is a function of your mental model and repertoire. Maybe putting pink polka dots on school notebooks aimed at girls seems obvious to a girl or to the parents of one (or to someone, like Clay Presley, coming out of the stationery business), but it was anything but obvious to competitors in the paper business with a "paper by the pound" mentality. Any hypothesis worth its salt generally leaves the uninformed and less prescient scratching their heads early on. The eureka comes later.

4. **A good hypothesis is *worth the trouble* to test.** In other words, the payoff is at least potentially worth the

effort, given that you have limited time and resources. Once you succeed at seeing differently and uncovering your customers' unarticulated needs, you are going to have more potential growth candidates than you can handle. You'll need to prioritize.

Prioritizing at this early stage is a risky business. It is difficult to assess accurately the true potential of an idea until you've taken it through some early moves. We're sure that there's a stack of PowerPoint files somewhere in the old Compaq archives demonstrating conclusively that Dell's idea of a direct-to-customer customized PC was a small and insignificant market opportunity, not worth riling Compaq's entrenched distributor network to pursue. So tread cautiously here. As we noted earlier, if the big ideas looked big at the outset, someone would have pursued them already.

Having said that, when you need to prioritize, the question of future scalability is an important one. Keep in mind that the impetus for starting small through learning launches is *not* to find opportunities to provide customized solutions to a small, specialized customer segment. That may be a perfectly attractive opportunity to pursue, but it is not the purpose of learning launches. Learning launches *start* small, but they don't want to stay that way. The aim is to produce new business ideas that can quickly be ramped up to significant volume, once you've got the recipe figured out.

Now that you know what a good hypothesis consists of, it's time to lay out the one that you've developed for your growth idea. We'll call it your "business concept." This template will walk you through the questions you must answer in order to create it:

Worksheet #1
BUSINESS CONCEPT

Describe (in as much detail as possible)

Customer Value Proposition

Describe the value proposition

Identify a *specific targeted customer.*

Describe this customer's *specific needs* and the way in which this new offering meets them better, faster, or cheaper than existing alternatives.

Capabilities

Identify the components of the value proposition that you will need to create and deliver

What *internal capabilities* does your idea leverage?

What capabilities are missing that you must obtain?

How and where will you obtain these?

What role do value chain partners have to play?

Competitors

Identify the current competitors in the marketplace

How will they react?

STAGE 3: ARTICULATING ASSUMPTIONS

So now you have immersed yourself in today's reality and generated your business concept, carefully and comprehensively. But of course there is a lot that you don't know as you launch the new offering. The goals in this stage are (1) to be sure that key "truths" are not actually assumptions *masquerading* as truths, and (2) to wade through the uncertainties and unknowns, separating those that *matter* from those that don't. You need to drill down to the core set on which the attractiveness of your new business concept depends. It is now time to articulate the *key assumptions*—to identify what you think, but don't know for sure, about three crucial elements:

- **Customers:** *How this offering creates superior value for them; why they will try it.*
- **Execution:** *How you will create and deliver the promised value; why the value chain partners whose support you need will work with you.*
- **Competitive reaction:** *How competitors are likely to react and the implications of their reactions.*

These key assumptions revolve around a set of educated guesses you've made about the likely behavior of customers, competitors, and value chain partners, and about your own ability to execute. At this stage, we are going to make those guesses explicit and gather data so that you can evaluate the new business concept against the four "tests" we talked about earlier: *value, execution, scalability,* and *defensibility*. Those are the core issues involved in identifying and testing the attractiveness of your new business concept.

Unpacking *why* you believe what you believe is the

heart of what we're doing here. Our goal is to interrupt the kind of automatic-pilot operation in which it looks as if "gut feel" is all you've got to go on.

Stepping back to examine *why* you believe what you do is tough work. Most of us are not very good at identifying the assumptions underlying what we believe. We just *believe* it—and act accordingly. We expect others to see the world the way we do. And we get frustrated when they don't. This is lethal behavior in a growth leader—the good ones almost always see the world quite differently than managers in maintenance mode. Worse yet, their perspective on the world is often completely opposite that of the organization's designated doubters.

The beauty of the hypothesis-driven process is that the doubters become your friends. You should gather up as many of them as you can find to point out all of the holes in your argument. They are good at this; chances are that you are not. Glass-half-full people desperately need the half-empty ones to help them do this work. So invite them into this conversation with enthusiasm.

When they are finished poking holes in your possibility, ask them to help you imagine the kind of *data* that would get them to change their views. Despite the fondness for analysis that exists in many large organizations, most of us are not very good at figuring out exactly what kind of data we need to test a given assumption. We are used to taking the information we already have and figuring out what it is telling us. But that happened in Stage 1. In Stage 3, we are working in the opposite direction: taking something we believe may be true and envisioning the kind of data we need to prove or disprove it.

These next questions will help reveal the key assumptions underlying your assessment of the attractiveness of your business concept:

The Value Test

How do you know that the customer has these needs?

Why do you think it is valuable to the customer to solve these needs?

How might you quantify this value?

What is the urgency of the need from the customer's perspective?

The Execution Test

Why do you believe that your firm is uniquely capable of producing the new offering?

What current capabilities are leveraged by the new offering?

What capabilities are missing?

Where will these new capabilities come from?

Which value chain partners do you need to cooperate?

Will they be interested? Why? What is the value proposition to them?

The Scale Test

Is this need specific to the particular customer, or does is it exist across a customer segment?

Is the specific customer need recurring or is it a onetime need?

The Defensibility Test

How will competitors react?

Which competitors are capable of copying the concept quickly?

How will you defend your position?

There is no substitute for engaging a diverse group of people in this conversation. Guard against spending your time talking only with people who are as excited about your idea as you are. Falling in love with your idea may be unavoidable; surrounding yourself with other lovesick puppies *is* avoidable. Keep in mind that the Catalysts excel at acknowledging the truth about reality while continuing to dream. This doesn't mean hanging out only with cynics who drain your energy and enthusiasm. It does mean listening carefully when people bring you what looks like bad news. Working only with people who think like you do is a waste of time. Groupthink is the enemy.

Now it is time to identify the assumptions underlying your business concept, the kind of data that you'll need to test them, and where you will find such information. Completing the next worksheet will help you to do this:

Worksheet #2
TESTING ASSUMPTIONS

Categories	Assumptions to be tested	New data that would change assumption	Source of data
Customers			
Capabilities			
Competitors			

STAGE 4: LEARNING LAUNCH

Now that you've identified your assumptions, it is time to design and then begin the learning launch itself. Remember that the purpose of the launch is to combine traditionally separate stages: validation and testing of the business concept, and a small-scale launch in the marketplace. Your goal is to generate data and insights quickly from direct market experience that allow you to test the key assumptions underlying the business concept. Think back to John Zahurancik and the initial moves he made to assess the promise of delivering broadband over AES power lines in Venezuela. He estimated that he needed to gain one hundred customers in the early move, he articulated in advance the key questions that needed answering, and he identified the data needed to do so.

Accomplishing this goal will involve pinpointing as precisely as possible the data you need in order to test your assumptions, and then creating a work plan for how you will generate those data. A key aspect of this is identifying who is likely to have the information you need and whom you will need to work with as part of the launch. Who might you approach as a potential customer? Collaborator? Value chain partner? Another important question to ask is how you will recognize success. What are the specific behavioral metrics you'll pay attention to?

As you design the launch, you will want to be explicit about the search for *disconfirming* data. These are the data that disprove your hypothesis. They are the most valuable data you can find—and the easiest to miss. To enhance your ability to detect this kind of information, you must lay out in advance—for each assumption—exactly what such disconfirming data would look like.

Finally, the details of the launch should also include timelines and resources needed—the basics of a typical project-management work plan. The worksheet below suggests a format for laying out your launch:

Worksheet #3
LEARNING LAUNCH PLAN

Timeline		
Activity	Partners Involved	Resources Needed

STAGE 5: REVISING THE BUSINESS CONCEPT

In some ways, the revision stage is the easiest of all. It involves taking what you've learned from your initial set of moves, reevaluating the attractiveness of the business concept, and then deciding whether to continue or halt the launch. If the initial assumptions underlying the attractiveness of your idea appear to hold true, you will want to move to the next set of launch steps, iterating and improving your hypothesis as you go. If, however, the idea fails key tests, it will be important to alter the hypothesis significantly before moving forward. It may even be necessary to "call the baby ugly"—or at least defer further action until a better hypothesis becomes evident, just as Conrad Hall did when his initial high-end recruiting publication failed to pass the value test.

Keep in mind that the goal here is not to be proven right—it is to learn how to make your business concept better. Pay special attention to data that "don't make sense" instead of discarding them. Embracing data that don't fit with your current worldview can be the key to achieving a breakthrough, higher-order solution.

As the learning launch progresses, you will need to incorporate a design for the upcoming scaling process and identify the new set of assumptions associated with it that will need testing.

STAGE 6: SCALING

At this stage, after multiple iterations and continued refinements to your business concept, you will have deciphered the recipe for success and be confident about your ability to accelerate your efforts and change your focus from learning to growing volume rapidly. This involves a different set of issues, such as how to achieve broader customer "uptake" quickly. Chances are that you have made your initial moves with a small and strategic set of partners. Now you will need to test approaches that help you reach a larger group of customers. Similarly, new issues arise on the execution side because meeting cost targets becomes more important.

You may also need to consider when, as the proud parent, you let the baby leave the nest. Sometimes the growth leaders in our study stayed on to manage the new business as it grew, integrating it into a larger business unit. Other times, they handed it off and moved on to new adventures. Regardless, an important part of the ultimate success of your initiative is building the relationships necessary to make the transition to scale a smooth one.

Enough already. Time to get to work. Since we know *not* to expect you to get it right the first time, you had better get started!

POSTSCRIPT

___

Advice to the C-Suite on Growing
Growth Leaders

In this postscript, we want to talk to the set of leaders we've ignored during the rest of this book: senior managers occupying the C-suite. No one would blame you for feeling a tad defensive at this point. After all, we've pretty much devoted the last eight chapters to coaching your managers on how to set up a kind of guerrilla organization for growth right under your nose—but also under your radar. We've tried hard to convince them to stop looking up to you for benediction and to look inside themselves instead, to stop whining and start doing, and to focus on creating better value for customers rather than running more numbers for Corporate. We've told them that the tug-of-war between stability and innovation is inevitable; that you—like Corporate—are sworn to uphold the systems and processes that keep the existing business humming along in a predicable way. We've advised them to give up hoping you'll be a better parent for growth and to use their energy to grow their businesses rather than fight for the transformation of their organization.

This is, in fact, what we learned from our three years

of research. After all, we never set out to find answers for *you*. We went looking for answers in spite of you. But we realize that you are on the firing line, too, expected to deliver growth along with stability. We suspect that many of you are already aware of what we've said here—that the organization you lead is getting in its own way. That the problem isn't just demanding shareholders, aggressive competitors, and low-growth markets. The problem is also, in part, *your organization*. And we suspect that you're not really all that unhappy with our advice to managers to end-run the system you oversee. You know that business as usual won't produce the top-line growth you need. You know that your numbers people are better at saying no than yes, and that while they may be the ones who help you make the quarter, they're not the ones building your future.

If you could find more of the kinds of Catalysts we've introduced in this book—more Kurt Swoggers, Jim Steiners, John Haughs, and Arkadi Kuhlmanns—you'd hire them in a minute. But although natural Catalysts are easy to spot, there are just not enough of them to go around. It's like holding out for Tiger Woods on your scramble team at the company golf outing. Even if you successfully recruit a Catalyst, there's a good chance that person won't stay for long, because most established organizations repel natural Catalysts the way antibodies repel a virus.

If you could grow your own Catalysts in a reasonable amount of time, you'd do that, for sure. Organizations such as General Electric nurture high-potential young managers through exposure to multiple businesses and functions, thus instilling the kind of broad repertoires and business acumen that our Catalysts developed on their own. But such thoughtful development processes take time—decades, really. Your successor will thank you for it. But what about today?

We suggest that you consider following the same advice we've given your managers: work with the resources you already have. This means finding Catalysts among the managers in your organization right now. Of course, as we've explained to these Catalysts-in-waiting, the choice to become a growth leader is *theirs,* not yours. But you can play a crucial role in accelerating their ability to succeed.

Since we completed the research for this book, we've met some C-suite executives who have embraced that role. Not surprisingly, it is tough work, requiring a willingness to face some harsh realities about what stands in the way of growth and then to do something about those obstacles. As always, that old "walk the talk" part turns out to be depressingly significant. Chances are, your people already hear you *say* growth but don't see you and your senior team *doing* what it takes to achieve it.

Let's look at Nick Liparulo, an executive who figured out both how to unleash the Catalysts in his midst and how to ensure that the organization would work with them instead of against them. Liparulo is the vice president of Westinghouse Electric's Engineering Services (WES), which performs maintenance and upgrade functions for nuclear power plants. Liparulo's staff read about our research with growth leaders and called us in the spring of 2006, interested in learning more. They were looking for a university to work with on the topic of organic growth and liked what we were doing; we were excited about finding a corporate partner to test-drive the new tools and approaches that we were developing through our research on the Catalysts. It was a match made in heaven.

Except that it kept our team up at night. Everything we knew about growth told us that it required dealing well with uncertainty and taking managed risks. We suspected—*hoped* in fact—that these weren't qualities common in the engineers who built and serviced nuclear power plants. Becoming growth leaders, we worried, would take a stretch so big and unfamiliar that we wondered if anyone with a background like theirs could pull it off.

Liparulo was willing to try. A Westinghouse veteran, he had watched the company shrink from a major diversified corporation that once rivaled General Electric to a nuclear power business owned by a British government agency, BNFL. When Liparulo stepped in to head WES, he was not surprised to find a mindset of complacency and a business model fast approaching its saturation point:

> The organization had been flat for so long and risk averse for so long that even getting us to go after any new business at all was an issue. We were in very specific areas comfortable to us. We were very busy. We seemed to be doing well. But we had a limited market. We were servicing nuclear power plants, primarily in the U.S. You can only do certain jobs a certain number of times. Our business is large plant changes, onetime changes. Sometimes you can tweak it a second or third time, but you run out of what you can do. It was clear to me that we had a problem, that our business was going to go flat. Looking ahead, the *best* we could do unless we changed something was stay flat.

No one had built a new nuclear plant in the United States in more than two decades. Ironically, the resurgence of interest in nuclear power, which could lead to the construction of new plants, was likely to exacerbate

WES's problem in the short term even though it was a boon to the Westinghouse parent company. Upgrades to existing plants would become less attractive and the nuclear engineering experts whom WES depended on could be lured away.

Recognizing the need to expand the WES business model and develop new sources of revenue growth, Liparulo and his strategic planning head, Bruce Monty, initiated a series of moves. But progress was slow, as Monty pointed out:

> We formed growth initiatives and had some growth leaders identified. We were tracking actions. But they were narrow. It just didn't seem like there was commitment. It was like, "OK, we've got to do this." But it wasn't a big deal. Nick said, "We've got to make a bigger deal of it."

Liparulo believed that the place to start was with his own team:

> People must first believe they have a problem. Where does that start? That started with my leadership team. We needed to acknowledge, collectively, that we did not want to lead a business that was not going to grow. Once we got past that, it wasn't hard to get the whole team to show up, because we had crossed the bridge. Then the question became *how* to grow. Once we started asking how to grow and looking for partners to help us, we were past the most important part. But the first part was to admit we had a problem, one that we didn't know how to solve.

The senior team knew that WES had a culture of risk-averse order takers. They needed to encourage a customer-centric culture with a sense of confidence—and urgency—around achieving growth. But they needed more than a change in perspective and ambitions; they needed new capabilities as well. Most of their managers, Monty worried, even if *committed* to the need for growth, simply had no idea how to get there.

Then came the acquisition by Toshiba in 2006, in which the diversified global giant and its minority partners paid $5.4 billion for the Westinghouse nuclear business. Anxious to recoup the premium paid, Toshiba soon set ambitious growth goals for its new U.S. subsidiary and expressed a willingness to support growth programs.

It was clear to Liparulo that they needed to move aggressively, but *how* to move was the issue. "That's where we were two years ago," he explained. "We were sitting here trying to figure out what to do and how to do it." He and HR manager Sally Maybray recognized that they needed help. They needed to learn about themselves to see if they could become growth managers, and they had to acquire some new tools for growing a business.

And that is why the entire WES senior group—comprising forty-five managers, most of them engineers—assembled in a Darden classroom in Charlottesville, Virginia, for a week in October 2006 to talk about growth and how to pursue it. Being engineers, they had carefully specified the new ways of thinking, leading, and behaving they hoped to achieve:

WES GOALS FOR THE DARDEN PROGRAM: WHAT WE'D LIKE TO LEAVE DARDEN WITH . . .

New ways of *thinking*:

- Recognition that growth is *everybody's* job, and driving it is core to all executives' roles
- An understanding of the competitive threats we face and the need to compete aggressively

---

- **A mentality of proactive problem solving that moves beyond silo thinking and reacting to customer requests to an enterprise perspective that anticipates customer needs**

New ways of *leading*:

- **The ability and confidence to motivate staff to think strategically about organic growth**
- **A toolkit of methods and frameworks to help generate, evaluate, and implement new opportunities**
- **Identification of needed changes in organizational infrastructure to better support growth, including identification of gaps, inhibitors, or barriers in current structure, systems, incentives, capabilities, and resources**

New ways of *behaving*:

- **Understanding of best practices followed by growth leaders in other mature businesses**
- **Identification of a set of concrete, specific, actionable high-priority next steps and deliverables post-Darden for program participants, both individually and as a group**

Also being engineers, they left Charlottesville with a plan and the resolve to implement it. Together, they created a kind of manifesto—their six strategies for getting to growth:

1. Execute flawlessly on current projects – DELIVER ON WHAT WE HAVE

2. Take maximum advantage of emergent opportunities / innovation in our primary market – SPEED KILLS THE COMPETITION

3. Leverage Toshiba products and services in the regional markets we currently serve – NEW PRODUCTS IN CURRENT MARKETS

4. Utilize global core competencies and products to serve targeted underserved regional markets, e.g. France, U.S. A/E market, U.S. BWR, Japan PWR, South Africa – CURRENT/NEW PRODUCTS IN NEW MARKETS

5. Implement a global resource strategy – "WIN THE WAR ON TALENT"

6. Selected acquisitions and alliances – BUY VERSUS MAKE WHERE APPROPRIATE

Liparulo then went back to Monroeville, Pennsylvania, and harnessed the organization's processes and systems to *support,* rather than obstruct, growth. Two years later, the difference is startling. As *BusinessWeek*[*] noted:

> The challenge is a familiar one: A big, hidebound company wants to be more creative. But Westinghouse has taken a somewhat unusual route to transcend its limitations: using the very processes its engineers are comfortable with—metrics, Six Sigma—to get workers thinking differently while at the same time minimizing culture shock. . . . [It is] a clever bit of organizational jujitsu.

The story of Liparulo and his team at WES is different from the other growth stories we've told in this book. It's not just a story about how individual leaders create top-line revenue growth—it's about how the organization can help. The code that Liparulo has cracked is not about getting to growth *in spite* of the organization—it's about designing an environment where corporate Catalysts work *hand in hand* with the organization.

APPLYING OLD LESSONS,
CREATING NEW ONES

The techniques the WES growth leaders used are pretty much the same ones we've talked about throughout this book. To start, they examined themselves as individuals. Each engineer took the DiSC instrument and learned—no surprise here—that as a group they were unusually high on the Conscientiousness dimension (but high on Dominance as well). They came to realize that the conscientiousness that was so critical in their technical work as nuclear engineers could, in fact, be a hindrance in their role as growth leaders. They recognized, as a group, that a mindset geared toward learning, rather than avoiding errors, was crucial on the business side.

They incorporated the elements associated with managing risk—leveraging existing capabilities, making affordable-loss investments, co-creating with customers—into their approach. The idea of leveraging existing technology turns out to be ideally suited to the nuclear industry, where customers prefer to use tried and tested technologies rather than take a risk with unproven approaches.

Though nuclear industry customers, accustomed to a traditional bid process, were reluctant to make pre-commitments, the bid process itself presented some interesting opportunities to experiment with small bets when the WES team reframed it as a learning process. Bruce Monty noted:

> The whole concept of affordable loss is that you need to be able to say, "I'm going to bid this new thing. Chances are, they'll tell me that they don't want it. But the next time, I'll adjust." You don't really know until they say, "We've picked this company to do this work." *Then* you

can analyze it and say, "Well, this was our approach. It wasn't right." It would be nice if we could sit down and design something together. But a lot of these guys don't want to get too close yet. They don't want to give any-body an advantage. So you've got to just go through the process of learning through bids.

Action was a byword Liparulo already believed in, so adopting a "small bets fast" approach was a no-brainer for him:

The worst thing to do is sit still. People will never rally around that. When you make a decision to do some-thing, people feel that. You can analyze this stuff for-ever. You have to do some analysis to make sure you're doing the right things, but at some point you have to make a decision and get on with life. It's usually cheaper to go out and find out that it really isn't a good area than to continue analyzing it for a year.

Even more interesting than their success at applying our growth code was the way Liparulo and his team taught us some new lessons. The most important was about align-ment. From the outset, the one idea that Liparulo refused to buy was our "under the radar" approach:

You can do growth under the radar, but my belief is that you're better off if you, as a leader, get alignment up, down, and sideways. Think of what you can accom-plish that way instead of trying to do something sort of undercover. You can accomplish so much more, so much faster, and your people can get so much more positive recognition, which energizes them.

Facilitating growth, Liparulo demonstrated, requires several different kinds of alignment. Growth starts with aligning the senior management team around what it really wants to accomplish and then bringing the rest of the organization into alignment with that intent. It requires alignment between those aspirations and the structure, systems, and processes to attain the growth the team needs to achieve. It requires alignment between what senior managers say they want and where they put their resources. Finally, growth depends on aligning the expectations of senior managers with a new experimental mindset.

Let's look at how each of these played out at Westinghouse.

As we've said, Liparulo focused on aligning senior staff with a vision for growth. Consider how the WES controller, Kathy Kovacic, described her role:

> Although my title is controller, my role is not just finance. Sally Maybray's role is not just HR. We are strategic business partners in this overall journey that we're making as an engineering service organization to grow the business.

This strategic partnership mentality produced benefits far beyond the ideological—they went to the very heart of why growth leaders at WES didn't need to operate under the radar. Think about it. Growth gridlock happens because of the disconnect between the systems controlled by the designated organizational doubters (often in Finance, but also in HR, IT, Legal, and other staff roles), all focused on stability, predictability, and the needs of a growing business for speed and the ability to learn in the marketplace. When the designated doubters become strategic partners who see their role as supporting growth rather than enforcing systems to the letter of the law, the possibilities for working within existing systems increase exponentially. It is the doubters who know the system best and are most capable of repurposing it to accomplish new things. Having them on your side makes a world of difference.

If your systems and processes make it as cumbersome to place a small bet as it is to place a big one, you are never going to move the needle on growth using the approaches outlined in this book, unless your managers end-run those systems. Therefore—ironically—the systems designed to facilitate corporate control actually reduce it by forcing growth leaders to subvert them in order to achieve the flexibility they need.

On the other hand, if you find ways to direct existing processes *at* growth objectives, your managers won't have to end-run them, and you'll be way ahead of the game. But this isn't easy—it takes a level of creativity and knowledge equal to identifying and executing the growth initiatives themselves. This was where WES really taught us a valuable lesson: The people *most* capable of pulling off this feat are the ones who own the systems. When they are designated doubters, this is a big problem; when they are strategic partners, this is a big opportunity.

Kathy Kovacic, in her role as a controller, understood how to make the Westinghouse financial system work for, rather than against, growth. She saw the opportunity to sell the entire growth effort as part of a *package,* part of the larger Westinghouse corporate financial planning process. This gave the corporate green light to the larger effort in a one-shot deal, and gave business unit management the ability to move quickly on specific decisions *within* the system. To achieve this, Kovacic asked the leaders of growth initiatives across WES to estimate four broad categories of costs: innovation funding needed for R&D, capital funding needed for asset investment, costs of implementation, and required headcount increases. They also estimated how much they thought they could grow the top line over the next five years. They then aggregated the admittedly crude estimates and incorporated them into the five-year financial plan. Kovacic explained:

> We presented the five-year financial plan to the leaders in this company: Nick's boss and his boss's boss. We said, "We think we can grow our top line, our revenues, by X-fold with these growth leaders. But guess what? It's going to require an investment. And here's what your return will look like." And we got complete endorsement to do that through our financial planning process.

Perhaps most impressive was WES's ability to harness Westinghouse's well-financed and deeply embedded corporate-improvement program, Customer First, to drive growth. Customer First uses traditionally efficiency-based tools such as Six Sigma and lean manufacturing, but the senior team at WES saw an opportunity to redirect these toward growth. Again, Kovacic explained how and why they took this approach:

> We used Customer First funding to enable us to work on projects that we felt were important. At the beginning of the year, as an engineering organization, we allot so much money per year to Customer First projects. Using Customer First to fund the growth initiatives was a very creative move. In an engineering company, nobody does anything without a shop order or a place to charge their time. We also used Customer First to look at these growth initiatives because we wanted the discipline of the process. Customer First is pretty rigid. There's a format that you have to follow. So the growth leaders had to come in to reviews with

Nick, Bruce, me, and their sponsor and review what they had learned, what their implementation plan was, and what their control plan was—meaning, How do I know if I'm on the right track? What are some of the things that I expect the rest of the organization to help me do to make sure I'm on the right track? We asked them to put some metrics out there for themselves, how they would define success.

It's been very clear to the growth leaders what their role is and how we were going to operate these as Customer First projects. And they had the full-time use of Customer First leaders to help them work through certain processes, especially creating business plans.

The Customer First process also enabled us to tell them if we felt they were on the right track—here's what we think is working, here's what we don't think is working. And people understand that if this is a Customer First project, and they're on that team, they need to go to the meetings.

Imagine people actually showing up to meetings on new growth initiatives because they thought they had to. That might be the most dramatic growth accelerator of all, as any leader who has suffered the tyranny of the "meeting missers" knows all too well. Time and time again, the folks at WES used the things that get in the way in other organizations as assets in their growth efforts. Even the Westinghouse hierarchy was made to work for, instead of against, the growth initiatives, as Kovacic noted:

Westinghouse is a very hierarchical organization. People look to the senior vice presidents: The rest of the organization usually lines up behind whatever they respond to and endorse. We've done a pretty good job in the past eighteen months of communicating Nick's support. He has talked about this in all employee

meetings, we've sent communications out, we've interviewed some growth leaders in our employee publications. In a big company like Westinghouse, you have to
make whatever you're trying to do very visible to the
organization. If it's well communicated and well understood and Nick endorses it, then people are more likely
to embrace it.

In addition, senior leaders walked the talk—they provided resources. At WES, this consisted most prominently
of a willingness to hire new talent instead of expecting
people to pursue growth in their spare time. Particularly
important was the creation of dedicated growth-leader
roles focused on developing new business in nine areas
that WES had identified as having high potential for organic growth. Kovacic again:

So often what happens is people are told, "We want
you to go work on this," but we don't take them out of
their current jobs, we don't fully dedicate them, we
don't give them money, and we don't make a big deal
about it. "Do this in your spare time but still do your
full-time job." Growth is just not going to get attention
that way.

Knowing that the group was unlikely to sell customers
something new unless they were already satisfied, WES
made executing current projects flawlessly their first priority. But Liparulo also worried about successful execution
of the new projects: "Suppose we were successful, suppose
we started winning all this stuff. Do we have the infrastructure to deliver?" In order to be prepared, he and his
staff concluded that WES needed an organization of project managers.

Creating that organization meant hiring in advance of

demonstrated business. This was a break with tradition. "Back in the 1980s and the 1990s, the nuclear industry wasn't growing. We were shrinking and doing a lot of layoffs. And so hiring in advance of actually having work was seen as a huge risk," Liparulo explained. Now he figures that WES can find some kind of work—even if it's not on the growth project they started on—for any of the smart people they hire. This attitude represents a large cultural shift. A case in point was the decision, made with uncommon speed, to open an office in San Jose, California. After GE announced the shutdown of its facility there, WES took advantage of the opportunity to attract a large cadre of seasoned GE nuclear engineers who were not interested in relocating. In the space of less than two months, WES made the decision to open the office and went on to hire more than twenty ex-GE engineers. This new willingness to take on selected risks was also evident in senior management's attitude toward losses in the bid process for new initiatives. Here again, the emphasis was on getting out there and trying, and on separating career and project success. Liparulo commented:

> We lost our first bids. So what? The growth leaders were more disappointed than I was because I didn't think we'd win. We wanted them to *try* to win, but as you work in this area you learn more and more and more. So you make more informed decisions. Until you're out there in the marketplace, you can do a lot of studies but you won't be as informed as if you're out there and competing. The risk is different on something we haven't done versus something we've done many times. And the probability of success is different. So you've got to be willing to take that risk. The challenge is if you put all that risk in a bid, you probably can't ever win the bid.

If I kill the guy who failed, then nobody's going to want to sign up to be a growth leader. All challenges are not equal. Growing an area is usually more difficult than running an area. These are good people. We picked good people and if someone isn't suited for the growth job, well, he'll still have *a* job.

WES leadership made action their mantra, recognizing that only dramatic action on their part would get taken seriously, as Bruce Monty noted:

We had a very bad time in the 1990s, when we were laying people off. We were hunkering down. In order to change that attitude, you can't just talk, you have to *do* stuff, like name growth leaders and spend some money. Then people see actions, and they get on board. You've got to shake things up. And I think that's what we've been able to do. That's why the attitudes changed.

Perhaps the most obvious evidence of the change to an outsider is the sense of confidence that the WES team members exude—a far cry from the "deer in headlights" paralysis evident when we met them. "We're on the right path," one growth leader explained to us, "and we're comfortable that we can figure it out as we go."

For Liparulo, it's the feel of the place that is most different:

Today, we have a sense of *energy* about growth that we didn't have before. I think that's helping us as much as the specific growth initiatives. The initiatives we are now pursuing are just demonstrations that we will commit to grow. I think we picked some pretty good areas, but time will tell. You make your bets, and some win and some lose. And you have to start over again in areas that lose. But what's really important is this sense of energy about growth. Five years ago, the idea was if we stuck to our knitting, but stayed flat, that was success. I don't think anyone here sees that as success anymore.

CRACKING THE GROWTH CODE
FROM THE TOP DOWN

The jury is still out on revenue growth at WES. It is a business with a long lead time; top-line sales results from some of the new growth initiatives are still several years away. But initial results are promising. Targeted growth areas, such as servicing competitor-built reactors that use an alternative technology, are well under way. Eighteen months in, top-line and bottom-line growth at WES are both up more than 20 percent.

Liparulo's story suggests some interesting directions for senior executives thinking about kick-starting the growth engine in their businesses. Here are the initial ones we see:

Look in the mirror: How committed to growth, and aligned in support of it, is your senior team? Not in theory, but in the reality of the hard choices that get made when the demands of existing and new businesses collide. Nick Liparulo lined up his own executives first and got their alignment on growth as a top priority. If your existing businesses get most of the resources and the best talent, go back to GO and do not collect $200. Solve that first or you will never get out of your own way.

Make allies of your designated doubters: This is not about encouraging staff to give away the store. Corporate

Catalysts aren't looking for sugar daddies; they won't ask for more than they need. Kathy Kovacic still guards the storeroom as ferociously as ever. But she also looks for ways to say yes instead of no, aware that replenishing supplies is also part of her job. Sally Maybray is still responsible for HR systems, but she also sees herself as a committed partner in the growth effort, responsible for attracting the new talent and skills needed. Give the people who have veto power over the things growth initiatives need a stake in making those initiatives succeed. Make growth *their* problem, and they will figure out how to be part of the solution. Who ever said accountants couldn't be creative?

Harness the power of embedded systems and processes to drive growth: Figure out how to make Six Sigma work for you on growth as well as quality and efficiency. Use your organization's obsession with metrics to shine the spotlight on growth. Rethink your strategic planning process and use it to prepare managers to recognize opportunity and help them think through and devise strategies for achieving growth. The revenue plug we talked about in chapter 1 needn't terrorize. It's a reality. But you shouldn't confuse handing your managers a plug with giving them a process that actually helps them grow their business.

Don't underestimate the power of focus: Mihály Csíkszentmihályi (he of *Flow* fame) argues that the most precious resource we've got is our attention. We can focus it like a laser beam and channel it to do powerful things, he argues, or dissipate it like a streetlight on a foggy night, casting only shadows. There is no doubt in our minds that focus really matters when it comes to growth and that when you divide a manager's attention between thinking about the future and fighting today's fires, the fires always win. Dedicate some resources to growth—100 percent.

Shelter new ideas, but not from the market: No matter how well you work to leverage existing systems and processes to support growth, sometimes you still need the protective bubble to keep the existing business antibodies from attacking the new initiatives. As the executive sponsor, you must be the ultimate guardian of growth. But while growth projects may need shelter from internal organizational demands, they must not be sheltered from external market realities. Throwing too much money at a new opportunity may have the unintended consequence of distancing growth leaders from the market they hope to reach. When you're sitting on plenty of cash, it can be easy to defer dealing with the reality of *real* customer demands. When you're short on cash, you are forced to go after customers first and listen hard to what they tell you.

Work to instill a love of learning in your organization: This learning isn't the kind you get in a classroom, but the kind you get in the marketplace. The values your people hold about learning determine whether you've got what it takes to succeed in the uncertain world of growth. Reduce the costs of learning wherever you can. Separate career and project success. Reward calling the baby ugly when it is. Honor trying as well as succeeding. Console intelligent failure. Having an entire organization walking around trying to avoid looking stupid may *sound* like a good idea, but it is just about the dumbest thing you can do for the future of your organization.

ACKNOWLEDGMENTS

———

The original catalyst for our work on growth was Frank Batten Sr. Both the motivation for this research and the funding to support it came from Frank Batten and the Batten Institute, which he established at the University of Virginia's Darden Graduate School of Business. We are forever indebted to him for his generosity and insight.

We would also like to thank former Darden dean Bob Harris, who believed in this project from its inception, and the current dean, Bob Bruner, who continued to support us. The other members of the original growth project team—Elizabeth O'Halloran, Sean Carr, Jim Mathews, and David Rippey—were wonderful colleagues who participated with us from the earliest stages of the research. Amy Halliday and Andrew King, our closest partners, contributed more to this work than can ever be acknowledged here. We are profoundly grateful to you. To all our friends at Darden and the Batten Institute, your vision to grow has been our guiding light.

Each of us has individual debts to acknowledge as well.

From Jeanne: My colleagues at Darden have been a source of inspiration, learning, and encouragement for the past twenty years, and I consider myself blessed to have spent my career at such an extraordinary place. To Salz, Miranda, Owen, Travis, Van, and all my beloved Loudkas, who bring such joy to every day.

From Bob: To Jay, Barbara, Dick, Randi, and the rest of my family and friends, who stimulate my mind and enrich my heart. To my colleagues at Healthy Companies International, who inspire me every day with wisdom, passion, and a commitment to excellence. Jim Mathews, David Rippey, and Rae Thompson are my real champions. Without them, this book would never be possible.

From Rob: With love always to Carla, Xavier, Mattie, and Nathan. To Warren Boeker, Nick Dew, Stuart Read, Violina Rindova, and Saras Sarasvathy; work would be just work without you. And to a tremendous project team with great colleagues. Life is a team sport.

INDEX

customers:
  assumptions about, 215, 218
  constraints of, 121
  "Cynthia-centricity," 103–4, 119
  deep knowledge of, 187, 199
  feedback from, 78–79
  focus on, 103–6, 119, 178, 184, 189
  learning from, 41, 45
  listening to, 105, 200
  modeling behavior of, 148
  as people vs. categories, 103, 104
  potential, 87
  precommitments from, 73–74, 77, 85–88, 99–100, 131, 211–12
  testing ideas with, 78
  in the value chain, 105
  value propositions for, 6, 84, 106, 108, 144, 178–79, 199
  working with, 42, 80, 83, 85, 119, 122, 166, 199
"Cynthia-centricity," 103–4, 119

Dahl, Roald, 191
data:
  analysis of, 9–11, 142, 143
  disconfirming, 219–20
  made-up, 10–11
  market sources of, 13, 74
decision-making, 40
  research on, 71
  seat of the pants, 142, 143
defensibility, 215, 217
Dell computers, 80, 109, 163, 213
denial, 147
designated doubters, 240–41
detachment, 57
digital light processing (DLP), 67–68, 90
DiSC Leadership Profile, 58
  average Catalyst scores, 60–61

dimensions in, 59–60
  questions about, 61
  Web offering of, 61
diversion, value of, 10
dominance, 59
doubt, 134–35
Dow Chemical:
  Polyethylene division, 176–78, 180
  Six Days in, 178
  Swogger in, 6, 18–19, 55, 140, 174–75
Dweck, Carol, 39, 43, 46, 48

Edelmann, Andrew, 110
education, changing mindsets through, 48
ego, becoming removed from, 57
entrepreneurs:
  affordable loss investing, 74
  as believers, 134–35
  facing uncertainty, 20, 45
  growing your business, 16–18
  hypotheses tested by, 24
  innovation by, 14
  learn-as-you-go, 42–43
  and learning launch, 24–25
  myths about, 68–70
  new sources of business sought by, 14
  pragmatic idealism of, 25
  shaping the future, 83, 92
  speed of, 186–87
  tactics of, 92–94, 122
  their own money, 91
  when to think like, 72
Ethel M, 30–36, 39
  chocolate lounges of, 32–34, 41, 87, 113, 131
  competition with, 31–32
  customer connection of, 42
  at Mars, 28, 31, 32, 34, 113
  partnerships in, 87

ABOUT THE AUTHORS

Jeanne Liedtka is a professor at the Darden Graduate School of Business Administration at the University of Virginia. Formerly the executive director of the school's Batten Institute, a foundation established to develop thought leadership in the fields of entrepreneurship and corporate innovation, Jeanne has also served as chief learning officer for the United Technologies Corporation, and as the associate dean of the MBA program at Darden. She has consulted with a wide variety of organizations and their leaders, from museums to law firms to large corporations, since beginning her career as a strategy consultant for the Boston Consulting Group.

Robert H. Rosen is chairman and CEO of Healthy Companies International (HCI), an executive consulting firm that advises companies in building healthy, high-performing organizations. As psychologist and business advisor, Rosen has interviewed more than 250 CEOs around the world and speaks to thousands of executives each year. He is the best-selling author of *Just Enough Anxiety*, *Leading People*, *Global Literacies*, and *The Healthy Company*. HCI'S clients include Northrop Grumman, ING, Johnson & Johnson, PricewaterhouseCoopers, and Merck. Rosen lives in Arlington, Virginia.

Robert Wiltbank is a partner of Buerk Dale Victor, a venture capital fund based in Seattle. He is also a professor of strategic management at Willamette University. His groundbreaking research includes the first empirical examination of the outcomes achieved by angel investors.